D

4

FAUST'S GOLD

ALSO BY STEVEN UNGERLEIDER, Ph.D.

*Health Resources Online: A Guide for Mental Health
and Addiction Specialists*
(with Colette Kimball, Laura Scheerer, Ph.D.,
Glenn Meyer, Ph.D., and Brian Zevnik, Ph.D.)

Mental Training for Peak Performance

*Quest for Success: Exploring the Inner Drive
of Great Olympic Athletes*

*Beyond Strength: Psychological Profiles
of Olympic Athletes*
(with Professor Jackie Golding)

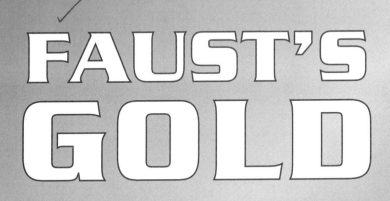

FAUST'S GOLD

INSIDE THE EAST GERMAN DOPING MACHINE

Steven Ungerleider, Ph.D.

THOMAS DUNNE BOOKS
ST. MARTIN'S PRESS ⁂ NEW YORK

THOMAS DUNNE BOOKS.
An imprint of St. Martin's Press.

www.stmartins.com

Library of Congress Cataloging-in-Publication Data

Ungerleider, Steven.
    Faust's gold : inside the East German doping machine / Steven
Ungerleider.—1st ed.
        p. cm.
    Includes index.
    ISBN 0-312-26977-3
    1. Doping in sports—Germany (East)   2. Anabolic steroids—Germany
(East)   I. Title.

    RC1230 .U544 2001
    362.29'088'796—dc21

                                                                2001017429

First Edition: June 2001

10   9   8   7   6   5   4   3   2   1

To the Franke and Berendonk family: you are the true heroes;

*To my girls, Sharon, Shoshana (PC), and Ariel (TB),
for holding down the fort and for your unconditional love
and support during these roller-coaster rides;*

*And to the memory of my parents, who taught me right
from wrong and who gave me the skills and courage
to step up to the plate when I need to!*

CONTENTS

ACKNOWLEDGMENTS

This was not an easy project. From the moment of inception to the last word, it was an enormous roller-coaster ride. Fortunately, I had a great ride, with lots of thrills and spills, and landed safely, with my feet planted squarely on the ground. There are many people I wish to thank: foremost let me begin with the athletes who were not only the heroes of this manuscript but real live people who struggle daily with the demons of their dark GDR history. I express thanks to Dr. Birgit Heukrodt, Rica Reinisch, Jutta Gottschalk, Sylvia Gerasch, Karen König, Catherine Menschner, Liesel Westerman Krieg, Carola Nitschke-Beraktschjan, Martina Gottschalt, Ute Krause, and Birgit Matz. A very special note of gratitude to Judge Hansgeorg Bräutigam of the Berlin District Court. And to many more who gave me some of their precious time to allow me to understand the GDR athletic machine.

I thank the following for granting me interviews under very difficult situations: Dr. Dorit Rösler, Dr. Jochen Kuehl, Dr. Harry Gordon of the U.S. Department of Justice office of the Drug Enforcement Agency, and to Ulrich Sünder. To the folks at St. Martin's Press, many thanks for your assistance and patience. This includes Peter Wolverton, Carolyn Dunkley, Barry Neville, and Bert Yaeger.

I also thank Marina Prufer for her great photos and court sketches, Jan Hegemann, attorney, and journalists Frank Bachner of *Der Tagesspiegel,* Hans Joachim Seppelt of SPF television, Marianne Heuwagen of *Zeitung,* Lars Broder Keil of *Atzte Zeitung,* Dirk Schmidtke, and Alan Maimon, Berlin bureau chief of the *New York Times*, and to Bob Voy, M.D.

Special thanks to my colleague and translator, Karin Fleischhacker, who made my job a whole lot easier, and to Ulrich Franke. And always a word of appreciation to my academic mentors, Professor Martin Acker and Dr. Milton Rosenbaum. And to my staff at Integrated Research, I thank all of you with heartfelt appreciation: Jan Bartunek, Colie Mason, Jerry Nordahl, and Colette Kimball. A special thanks to my dear friends of thirty-five years (yikes), Michael Levin and Stu Perlmeter, for all of your support while I write and don't answer your phone calls. Also, a note of appreciation is extended to lawyer Richard Young, assistant Peggy Winter, to my colleagues at Justice for Athletes, Bill Mason, Steve Baum, David Ulich, and a very special thanks to Dr. Alan D. Rothstein for your precious support.

Many thanks to Christian Paschen and to Berlin attorney Dr. Michael Lehner, who gave the victims of the GDR a voice and fought through the maze of the German legal system to bring about true justice. And to Professor Werner Franke and his wife, Brigitte Berendonk, for their gracious contributions of time and energy and support. They are the anchors and voice of truth for this project. Without their tireless efforts and perseverance, many more victims would have suffered.

To Alice Rosengard, a very special person with a great eye and outstanding intuition, a million thanks! You made this manuscript come to life and you are a pleasure to work with!

I also thank my colleague Dr. Gisela Ulich for her time and energy in translating many important documents and articles for me. Finally, I owe a huge debt of gratitude to my dear friend, German scholar, sports-law expert, and fellow sidewinder, attorney David Ulich of Sheppard Mullin, for his support, emotional encouragement, professional advice, and insight at many critical points along the roller-coaster ride.

PREFACE

During the 1970s and 1980s, East Germany's corrupt sports organization dominated international amateur athletics. In the three decades when the GDR's secret "State Planning Theme 14.25" was in effect, more than ten thousand unsuspecting young athletes were given massive doses of performance-enhancing anabolic steroids. They achieved near-miraculous success in international competition, including the Olympics. But for most, their physical and emotional health was permanently shattered.

Faust's Gold draws on the revelations of the ongoing trials of former German Democratic Republic (GDR) coaches, doctors, and sports officials who have now confessed to conducting ruthless and destructive medical experiments on young, talented athletes selected for the elite Olympic training camps. The book also draws on the extensive research of Brigitte Berendonk and her husband, Professor Werner Franke. Berendonk, herself a victim of the GDR's doping machine, escaped from East Germany to begin a decades-long crusade to bring justice to those who were not so fortunate. Her story and those of her fellow athletes in the GDR offer an unflinching view of life in an amoral totalitarian regime, as well as a true-life detective story in which she and Franke are pitted against a formidable opponent: the East German secret police, known as the "STASI."

These elements are woven into the complex tapestry of the politicized modern Olympics.

Over and above matters of sport and the culture of athletics, I have attempted to provide some insight into a nation obsessed with victory, no matter the cost. In following that obsession, the architects and agents of the GDR doping system forever altered our concepts of sportsmanship and competition.

FAUST'S GOLD

1

Prologue

In the late 1970s, I began to work as a sports psychologist with many elite athletes, some of whom went on to compete for our United States Olympic teams. Over the years, I kept hearing these athletes bitterly protesting the unfair advantage posed by the enormous change in the athletic prowess of the East German competitors, a change that observers assumed was due to some type of synthetic hormone.

"We would be in the locker room with these female swimmers," the U.S. athletes would tell me, "and we would have to check the symbol on the door to make sure we had the right bathrooms. These swimmers—they were huge. They had shoulders like Dallas Cowboys, hair growing all over their bodies. It was quite startling," they reported. Many swimmers who competed internationally commented that it wasn't just the physical attributes of the East German women that was troubling, but also their aggressive behavior. "They would spit on the floor," one swimmer told me. "They would look at you like they wanted to rip your tongue out. It was all a bit surreal, and very intimidating." The more complaints we heard, the more we coaches and consultants told our American competitors to "just stay focused, don't get distracted, and swim your best race; don't worry about the other folks."

In 1984, when I was appointed to the first sports medicine group of the United States Olympic Committee, I learned more about this issue. There were more rumors, more anecdotes, more drug testing, and speculation about the East Germans, but no proof. In the late 1980s a group of my colleagues went to Germany and met with officials in Leipzig, at the most prominent sports institute for GDR training. It was there that some "informal" documents surfaced that provided evidence that there really was a secret system in place to dope many GDR athletes. None of us had any idea of the scope of this plan, nor did we know that the dam was about to break.

Years later, when I read about the work that former Olympian Brigitte Berendonk had done, documenting years of GDR doping, I became intrigued. Several of my colleagues encouraged me to call Brigitte and her husband, a highly respected molecular biologist named Werner Franke. After many conversations by phone, we finally met in Berlin. We agreed then that a psychologist, a molecular biologist, and a former Olympian who was now a schoolteacher might make a good team for the purpose of collecting and disseminating information as it came to light. More important, we agreed that the story had to be told.

The Big Oak Room

The Thirty-fourth Superior Criminal Court of the Berlin
Landgericht is a massive neoclassical building of smog-
stained limestone block. The structure dominates the normally quiet streets of the surrounding Tiergarten. But on
the Wednesday morning of April 20, 1998, the street outside the courthouse was anything but quiet. Remote television vans top-heavy with antennae jostled for parking spots,
and a cluster of frustrated camera crews and still photogra-
phers shuffled in the chill spring sun, grinding their ciga-
rette butts on the marble entrance steps, much to the
chagrin of the police officers guarding the ornate bronze
doors. Although Germany's attention was focused on this
courthouse, cameras and microphones were excluded from
the proceedings taking place inside.

Room 700, a cavernous chamber with oak-paneled walls
and heavy rafters, was filled to capacity. Presiding Judge
Hansgeorg Bräutigam sat perched high above the other
adjudicators in a wooden boxlike structure. Three judges
and two laywomen jurors sat on the wide, varnished bench

that stood between two incongruous wood-and-glass cages, bulletproof witness stands built in the 1950s when the fledgling West German government continued the Nazi war crimes trials begun at Nuremberg in 1946.

The six defendants in Room 700 today, however, sat at tables in open court. This trial was the first in a series scheduled over the next two years to determine guilt of a different magnitude, but similar in nature to that of the Nazis. Almost fifty years after the Nuremberg trials had begun, the cruelty of another totalitarian regime, the communist Deutsche Demokratische Republik, had now come before the bench of justice.

The charges of Criminal Case 28 Js 39/97 were Willful Bodily Harm inflicted by the six defendants on children, including the three witnesses in court today. The indicted men were two medical doctors, Dieter Binus and Bernd Pansold, along with four coaches and trainers, Volker Frischke, Dieter Krause, Rolf Gläser, and Dieter Lindemann. All had been part of the swimming program of the Sport Club SC Dynamo Berlin in the 1970s and 1980s, when the state-run organization was the hub of East Germany's seemingly invincible elite athletic juggernaut. The specific accusations were that they had intentionally administered anabolic steroids and testosterone to nineteen unwitting, underage female swimmers between 1975 and 1989 in order to secretly and illegally enhance their performance—without regard for the well-documented serious health problems associated with these powerful drugs.

The three prosecution witnesses in this trial, Birgit Matz, Carola Nitschke-Beraktschjan, and Christiane Knacke-Sommer, sat with their attorneys at a separate table, behind the federal prosecutors. Twenty-five years earlier, they had been among the GDR's star teenage athletes, winning individual and team medals at the 1976 Montreal and 1980 Moscow Olympic Games. Now in their late thirties and early forties, the women were tastefully dressed in the subdued corporate mode of the prosperous 1990s European Union.

But when the prosecutors called Christiane Knacke-Sommer to testify, her well-tailored suit could not hide her unnaturally wide shoulders and powerful arms. Like the other witnesses in the case, she had been a normal, healthy pubescent girl in the mid-1970s. Then her family sent her to live and train at SC Dynamo to compete for the greater glory of the state. Now, three decades later, she spoke of those years in an unusually deep voice that was tense, yet controlled.

Among the spectators, listening intently to the testimony and imagining themselves in Christiane Knacke-Sommer's place, were other former GDR athletes. Their names read like an Olympic lineup: Birgit Heike Matz, Ute Krause, Rica Reinisch, Birgit Heukrodt, Karen König, Andreas Krieger, Martina Gottschalt, Jutta Gottschalk. Some were unsure whether they should testify, whether they *could* testify, knowing that it would be not only painful, but also dangerous to do so. All were aware that they might be called upon to come forward.

A prosecutor patiently led Christiane through the early years of her childhood in a small Saxon town near Dresden, then shifted to the months when she was first installed in the "swim club" dormitory and began her training regimen. SC Dynamo was a closed complex, she testified. The young athletes training there were isolated from their families and the outside world. Separated from her parents,

Christiane had turned thirteen while at SC Dynamo. After a thorough initial physical and psychological examination, the medical and athletic officials in charge of the establishment determined that she had potential as an Olympic-class butterfly swimmer. For the next two years, she steadily advanced in club competition, and was finally selected for the coveted elite group from which GDR Olympic team members would be chosen. This group of swimmers was the responsibility of Dr. Dieter Binus and trainer Rolf Gläser.

It was then that she was given the "little blue pills." Christiane's voice hardened as she continued her testimony. At first, she wasn't concerned about taking the small tablets, the innocent color of robin's eggs, which Rolf Gläser administered daily in strict four-week cycles. At the time, it did seem a bit odd that the trainer insisted that all the girls receiving these "special vitamins" swallow them in his presence. But Gläser dismissed the girls' concerns, pointing out that the "nutritional supplements" had cost the state too much to be wasted on careless adolescents who might forget to take them.

After two cycles, Christiane said, she felt the effect of the pills in both her performance and her body. While preparing for the European Championships in Sweden in 1977, Christiane was given a four-week course of both blue and pink tablets. Her qualifying time for the 100-meter butterfly race dropped dramatically. But she was startled by the equally dramatic and sudden increase of muscle mass in her upper body and arms. More alarming were the other physical changes. She developed serious acne. Her body hair increased dramatically, with pubic hair extending over her abdomen in a typical male pattern. Her voice broke into a gruff, bass timbre, like that of a young man. And her previously restrained libido, typical of girls in the puritanical GDR, flared wildly. These symptoms only worsened after Dr. Binus administered a painful injection in June 1978, just prior to the World Championships in West Berlin.

"Did defendant Gläser or defendant Binus ever tell you the blue pills were the anabolic steroid known as Oral-Turinabol?" the prosecutor asked. "They told us they were vitamin tablets," Christiane said, "just like they served all the girls with meals." "Did defendant Binus ever tell you the injection he gave was Depot-Turinabol?" "Never," Christiane said, staring at Binus until the slight, middle-aged man looked away. "He said the shots were another kind of vitamin."

"He never said he was injecting you with the male hormone testosterone?" the prosecutor persisted. "Neither he nor Herr Gläser ever mentioned Oral-Turinabol or Depot-Turinabol," Christiane said firmly. "Did you take these drugs voluntarily?" the prosecutor asked in a kindly tone. "I was fifteen years old when the pills started," she replied, beginning to lose her composure. "The training motto at the pool was, 'You eat the pills, or you die.' It was forbidden to refuse. But the pills and the shots, they destroyed me physically and emotionally."

Christiane raised her hand and pointed across the dark-paneled courtroom to the defendants' table. "They destroyed my body and my mind. They gave me those pills, the Oral-Turinabol, which made me crazy and ruined my body." Christiane glared at Dieter Binus; then her voice rose in fury. "They even poisoned my medal!" She suddenly stood and hurled to the floor the token of her supreme achievement, the bronze medal she had won swimming for East Germany in the 1980 Moscow Olympics. "It is tainted, poisoned with drugs and a corrupt system. It is worthless and a terrible embarrassment to all Germans."

Presiding Judge Hansgeorg Bräutigam gaveled the stunned courtroom to silence. But he did not admonish Christiane Knacke-Sommer. Everyone in Room 700 knew she had spoken the truth.

Neither spectators nor participants seemed to enjoy hearing the disturbing details of Christiane and the other former athletes' mistreatment at the hands of communist East Germany's vast and powerful sports apparatus, nor of the anguish they had suffered as a consequence. But the time was past due, as Christiane told the judge, for a "new honesty." And within weeks of the trial's completion, Christiane and her fellow witness Carola Nitschke-Beraktschjan, announced that they were returning all their competitive medals and requested that their names be removed from the official Olympic records.

As to the need for "a new honesty," no one in the courtroom could have agreed more fervently than Brigitte Berendonk, who was seated among the spectators. A tall woman in her late fifties, she still had the physique and carriage of a world-class athlete, as she had been. But few in attendance at the trial realized that this brave and resolute woman, more than any other individual, was responsible for bringing before the bar of justice over 400 doctors, coaches, trainers, and sports association officials of the Deutsche Demokratische Republik who had devised and administered the most massive and pervasive doping system in the history of competitive sport.

3

Baumausreissen

"When my father died, I went to his funeral, and I looked at his body and I thanked him for allowing me to leave the GDR," Brigitte Berendonk tells me. The former Olympic track and field star has agreed to join me to talk about her past at a Konditorei in the center of Heidelberg. "I uttered a silent prayer and praised him for getting me out of the filthy East, away from the doctors and trainers who were abusing us with drugs and their sick medical experiments." It is a bright, sunny afternoon in July of 1998. We sit outside, having our coffee and pastry, surrounded by fifteenth-century castles and other historical landmarks. As we speak, the doping trials are just getting under way in Berlin. "He wanted me to be okay with leaving the old Germany. My father knew too much about the corrupt system that was poisoning our minds and bodies . . . but he wanted me to be safe with the decision," she says.

Tall and slender, with an athletic build, Berendonk is still in excellent shape for someone nearing the age of sixty. No longer possessing the discus and shot-put physique of

Olympic proportions, she now has a more delicate and sober look. Her eyes are lively, her manner intense and engaging, as she tells how she came to be the hub of the doping victims' efforts at restitution.

Arriving in Mexico City in 1968 to compete for West Germany in the Olympics, she was startled by the changes in the GDR athletes. She knew, of course, what had brought on the masculine appearance, the arrogant and aggressive behavior, the excess body hair on these women. Then, when she competed in Munich in 1972 and was badly beaten by athletes who had obviously been doped with steroids, she reacted with outrage, insisting that something had to be done. She spoke out in protest of the doping and was ridiculed in the press. Undaunted, she continued to speak out. She was relentless.

It was well-known in the world of sports that Berendonk was the daughter of a doctor and that her former coach was a scientist as well. Consequently, she had substantial credibility among her colleagues. Many saw fit to confide in her about their own experiences. With the publication of her book on the subject, they came to her in increasing numbers, hoping to get the truth exposed to the public. As she was already in contact with lawyers on her own behalf, she was in the position of being able to direct other athletes to federal prosecutors. One by one, they told of their experiences as young athletes who were given powerful and dangerous substances without their knowledge.

In the beginning, she had been one of them.

"The GDR athletic system, it was all a big scam," she says. "For years I have had to live with these awful and painful secrets about what they did to us. You know, the victim always believes that [she is] deserving of the abuse; it is a well-known psychological profile." She looks at me as if I did know.

"And when I think about my years as an Olympian, both in my competition in 1968 in Mexico City and then in the Munich Olympics [when she took eleventh place], it seemed natural at that time that we all looked like well-trained athletes, conditioned athletes. But I knew deep in my soul that the doping was wrong. The GDR, the system that I escaped from, had created monsters. These were not real people, just engineered experiments," she says.

First a GDR athlete and later a defected West German Olympian, Brigitte Berendonk is bearing witness. Our eyes are locked in an intense gaze, and she seems to trust me. Periodically, people stop by to greet her; after all, she is a teacher who is well-known in this intimate community. Yet she barely misses a beat. She says a quick hello and comes right back to our conversation. Besides teaching and being a mother of two, she spends many hours each day as an advocate for German athletes. She is supporting the victims, those little girls, now women, who are scared, yet need to come forward to tell their stories. It cannot be easy, I think, to tell of the horrors of their bodily functions, of the changes in their sexual feelings, of being asked by a coach to abort their babies.

"I was at first upset about the cheating. It was no longer track and field and training and competition," she tells me. "It was no longer simple as to who the best was. It was gone, we lost the innocence of sport. And through my husband, a respected molecular biologist whom I met in 1966 and who was my coach [until they married in 1975], I learned that it was not sport, but really a form of science. Sport was becoming just a medical experiment, another German model of human engineering, and all of this was very dangerous to the body."

There is a slight tremor in her voice as she continues. "The whole business of virilization and how young ladies became masculine overnight, and what that does to the organs, especially the liver . . . this was so upsetting," Brigitte says quietly. "And then the doctors had the audacity to tell us that you could not detect these drugs in our system."

It is early evening and the sun is setting in Heidelberg. It has been a lovely July day, a bit cool, but splendid amidst the centuries-old buildings. Mark Twain came to Heidelberg to write; he stayed for quite a while. Goethe lived here, and Mozart traveled from Vienna to perform in one of the famous castles. Creative energy oozes from every pore of this city's long and storied life.

While we continue our conversation over dinner, surrounded by secret documents and good German wine, Berendonk describes a system that went off the deep end. "What we saw was lots of muscle mass, massive amounts of human tissue that had changed, calves like tree stumps, Achilles tendons like cables of a bridge," she recalls. "But the tendons do not adapt; they don't grow with the same strength and flexibility. They are a mismatch. Tendons tear; they don't grow in synch with muscles. Tendons seem to rip and fall apart with all of these steroids. Throwers had lots of injuries from the use of Dianabol, the drug of choice in the 1970s and 1980s. It was made by the pharmaceutical giant Ciba-Geigy. As muscles grew, the overall development did not work well with tendons; there were lots of serious injuries," she explains somberly.

The next day is stunning; we are met by a rich blue sky and fresh morning air. Brigitte and I go for a walk into the hills of Heidelberg, up a million stairs to a fifteenth-century castle, an historic site where Goethe used to come to contemplate his future. The city is bustling now; there is real energy and excitement here. Children are playing soccer in the streets, bouncing balls off the cobblestones, squealing with delight when they hit an innocent by-stander.

Brigitte looks heartsick as she speaks about the loss of sport and innocent play, recalling her restricted existence as a young athlete in the GDR's elite sports program. "We never talked about our bodies and the chemical changes. No one ever spoke; it was taboo. We never mentioned the dirty word of drug or steroid," she admits. "Germans don't talk, they just experiment, keep it inside themselves, and live with the pain. There is no 'open speak' among us, just lots of secrets. It was not okay to dope our athletes, and it was certainly not okay to speak about it. The secret was kept between the doctors and the athletes and the coaches. There were lots of victims"—she nods—"and there will be many more."

As we walk, we approach the home that she shares with her husband, her son, Ulrich, twenty-two, and daughter, Friederike, twenty-four. I keep firing the questions; answers are being returned in rapid succession. She seems to want to share more with me; it's as if no one has been willing to ask until now. Or perhaps no one has been allowed to question.

She tells me about a German track athlete, Ewe Beyer, a hammer thrower. Brigitte says that after he competed, he was invited to a televised debate with sports medicine officials about the GDR system. So he went on television with a prescription pad in his pocket, ready to confront his trainer and doctor. "If the doctor denies his doping practices, I will take out the px and expose the doctor on national TV," he declared. But, Berendonk laments, "this was the exception; it was rare to talk openly or with the media about our big, ugly German secret!" In 1993, Beyer died of a heart attack at the age of forty-eight.

Berendonk had lots of friends who were doped and fell ill. Most would not talk, but a few had sad stories to tell. One friend told her of a depression that he experienced. "He talked about the feeling of well-being when he was cycling on his steroids," she says, her eyes widening. "He would say that he felt invincible and that he could tear out a tree with all its roots; that was his strength. And whenever he walked into the arena he would feel this strong and this powerful. You feel that you can beat any competitor when you are doped . . . and in German we say: '*Baumausreissen,*' [Ripping up the trees]!

"But when he stopped taking the drugs," she says, "he went through a deep depression. He felt as if the walls and the roof were crashing down all around him. He had no energy and he felt awful when he came off the drugs. So he went to his doctor to explain the problem and the physician put him back on steroids!"

Brigitte seems a bit embarrassed for her fellow athletes. "Doctors can never be excused," she says emphatically. "It is a crime. Doctors knew this. Parents were lied to; they noticed the physical and emotional changes in their children and they asked why is my child looking different. The secret police files showed they were told to lie to all parents—to lie to everyone."

Berendonk is talking at a quick pace now, faster and

faster; she seems frustrated by not having the time to get it all out. "Some parents took their kids away, but you must know that in the GDR, your life was taken care of. Your studies, your house, it was all taken care of in the East," she explains, extending her hands into the air as if to say, yes, they were the good-hands people. "So many parents did not ask too many questions. We wanted the state to take care of us. In the East, eight years of school was compulsory, but to continue for four more after that, you had to have connections. In order to get more education, you had to believe in the socialist program, you had to play by the rules, be a part of the scene, their scene and their rules," she says angrily. "My father and mother were well educated, my father was a GP, a doctor with a good practice. So with me being a good athlete, they let me move ahead in the sport system."

She reflects for a moment before she continues. "I was a superb athlete, and I was invited to the training facility at Leipzig because I was very promising . . . and we were all tested," she says, looking away. "And they asked me what would I like to do after my sports career . . . they wanted to assure us that the state would take care of us. The East Germans . . . they were very seductive. If I didn't have athletic skills, then I would be sent back home. I would be nothing. The GDR wanted the superior human beings; the human engineering experiment was to locate and nourish the best and the brightest. They bribed us; it was coercion. They put us in the friendly prison," she says half-jokingly. "They wanted to reward us for performance so that the system could survive and flourish."

Brigitte is visibly upset. She looks deep into my eyes. "The system was obvious, but we didn't know yet that we were part of the *big* human experiment. Everything was done for us. You never know what lies in the background or how deceptive it is while you are in it," she says. Then she tells me of the move that saved her: "In the fall of 1958," she says, "I already knew that we, our family, would leave. I knew that we would defect to the West. I won the junior championship, and my parents knew that it was time."

"In September, our whole family, my parents, brothers, and sisters, we all sat and we talked about this. My mother confessed later that she had thought that maybe I would fight the system, and I would want to stay in East Germany. My mother knew that things were good for me . . . and that the state was looking after their prized athlete. But my parents did not want the family to be divided. They were worried about our future.

"My father had a chance to practice medicine in West Germany, so he went to Heidelberg to explore possibilities. As a family we wanted to agree; this was important for all of us," she recalls. "My father, the doctor, knew about the drugs, the doping of little girls, the virilization, and the human experiments. He knew the risks. He wanted to protect me. So, in December, we left the GDR, the evil system. We escaped in the middle of the night and went to the West," she says, looking toward the heavens.

"So, when my father died and I went to his grave to say good-bye," she says with tears welling up in her eyes, "I thanked him for making this critical decision and saving our family—saving my life."

Brave New World

Listening to Brigitte Berendonk tell of her family's difficult decision to defect to the West, I was reminded of just how different life had been in East Germany only a decade ago. What I was learning about the GDR doping program from the recently uncovered documents seemed to have come out of a whole other world. And, in a way, it had.

For three decades after Berendonk had left the GDR, the records detailing the crimes perpetrated against her and her fellow GDR athletes remained suppressed. In fact, until 1991, it was not even known that such records existed, because they had been secured by the secret police.

From its inception in 1949 as a puppet community for Moscow, the GDR had been a police state that suspended and revoked basic human rights, from elections to free speech. When its citizens tried to flee, it built a huge retaining wall to close them in. East Germany's government spied on most of its citizens almost daily. It has been reported that every seventh person was employed by the state; some 100,000 were members of the SED (Socialist

Unity Party) elite, ranging from high-security personnel to party politicos. Many of these citizens, including athletes and their families, were rewarded handsomely with stipends, spacious luxury flats, and automobiles.

The Ministry for State Security (Ministerium für Staatsicherheit), whose dreaded secret police were known as the "STASI," offered certain citizens special privileges in exchange for information and cooperation. When, on November 7, 1989, subsequent to widespread dissent and demands for reform, the politburo—the East German power structure—resigned, secret messages were being sent to the STASI to shred all sensitive documents, especially those which had contained information about domestic informers. Two days later, the Berlin Wall fell.

Many East Germans were appalled when they realized how badly they had been treated during the GDR regime. They had been controlled, manipulated, and impoverished by their own leadership. Their anger and resentment resurfaced when the press reported that their neighbors, friends, and professional colleagues had been spying on each other for years. As remaining documents from STASI headquarters revealed, informers had been instructed to watch every movement of their citizens in the interest of state security.

In 1991, a law was passed, somewhat akin to our Freedom of Information Act, that allowed citizens access to their files. Some five miles of shelves housed documents in the STASI ministry. This stack of papers has become known as the Gauck Authority, where some one million Germans have applied to see their personal files. Meanwhile, two million employers have asked for the removal of any colleagues who were found to have cooperated with the STASI. Not only have victims been able to search for and find the truth about themselves, but other matters of state security, including the systematic doping of nearly all elite athletes, have come to light.

Nonetheless, in 1994, on the eve of the opening of the Winter Olympics in Lillehammer, an opinion poll conducted in Berlin revealed that 57 percent of former East Germans advocated closing the STASI files. In 1997, ZERV, the special elite federal investigative unit designed to research STASI crimes and consisting of 270 detectives, closed its doors. Manfred Kittlaus, the former chief of ZERV, noted, "the majority of human rights violations will be beyond the law . . . the perpetrators will soon be free to walk down the street with impunity."

Despite this development, there was still great determination—especially on the part of Werner Franke—to find the evidence of what he and others had long suspected—namely, that physicians and trainers entrusted with the development of young athletes had been in league with the most ruthless forces of the communist regime. And while that partnership might seem shocking to citizens of a free society, it is not so shocking in the context of the GDR. That government was, after all, the product of two evil dictatorships, the Third Reich and Stalin's Soviet Union, and its history is buried in the deep wounds of World War II. The crimes of the STASI police—and of their accomplices in the doping program—were not remotely of the same magnitude as those committed by the Nazis. But the two regimes have a unique relationship, linked as they are by a sinister past.

In any case, as it eventually became clear, the East German government was deeply involved in the elite athletic program that it was controlling through the STASI police, and committed almost two-thirds of its precious resources to this program. One reason for these measures was that international sporting competition had become an arena of high visibility and prestige. East Germany viewed sport and competitive games as an opportunity to gain recognition on the international political stage, while offering its athletes a chance to bring glory to a nation in turmoil.

Ironically, around the time when the GDR doping program began, the Olympics were viewed as a bastion of impartiality, based as they were on the purest ideals of the most advanced Western civilization of ancient times.

The origins of fair play go back as far as the ninth century B.C., when the truce of "Ekecheria" was established by three kings, demanding that all of ancient Greece ratify a peace treaty so that athletes and artists could travel safely and compete without the fear of war and destruction.

While studying at the Sorbonne University in Paris in 1892, Pierre de Coubertin, a Frenchman and founder of the modern Olympics, conceived the international Olympic Games as a way to build a peaceful and more harmonious world by educating youth in the ways of sport, to be practiced without any discrimination and conducted in the spirit of cooperation and friendship, under the rules of fair play. In his academic proclamation, he envisioned the Olympic Games as a festival of sport and culture, combining strength, beauty, and ethics among people.

De Coubertin said that Olympic ideals and ethics could develop humanistic values for all, encouraging peaceful gatherings and providing nations with an opportunity to promote justice, democracy, and tolerance.

With the help of modern-day diplomats and later the United Nations, the international Olympic movement has intervened in many spheres throughout its century-long existence. There is no better example of this intervention than the Eleventh Olympiad, the Games that have become known as the Nazi Olympics. The National Socialist German Workers' Party had instructed their athletes to win and win big, so as to assert their political and social prestige in the international arena, where they had failed for so long. Hitler had demanded that the 1936 Olympics be a celebration of life and achievement. Using the resources of Dr. Carl Diem, the head of the organizing committee, Avery Brundage, the IOC chief and former diplomat, and the pre-eminent filmmaker and artist Leni Riefenstahl, Hitler promoted the agenda of the Third Reich under the guise of a festive environment. His intent was short-circuited when the gifted African-American track star Jesse Owens ran away with several gold medals, thus giving the lie to the notion of "white Aryan supremacy."

For forty years after the 1912 Stockholm Olympics, the Russians had boycotted the games. In 1952, they finally came back to the playing field, sweeping their first series of gold medals at the Helsinki Olympics. They won twenty-two gold medals, second only to the United States, thus creating the first cold war battle of sport. By 1956, having poured millions of dollars into sport programs, the Russians had achieved their goal and were top dogs in the medal count.

In 1972, Munich was the host city for the Olympic Games. Not wanting to repeat the highly politicized agenda of the 1936 Olympics, the German government attempted to put on a world-class sporting event. Drug testing was just beginning, so no valid instruments were available to detect anabolic steroids. (That came later, in 1976.) But other drugs—including amphetamine-look-alike compounds—were being tested for.

Unfortunately, the gold medalist and world record holder, sixteen-year-old swim sensation Rick DeMont of the United States, tested positive for ephedrine, a drug that had been preapproved for use in his asthma medication. This unpleasant episode (which is still being reviewed in the American courts some twenty-eight years later) was overshadowed by the murder of eleven Israeli athletes, who were ambushed at midnight by the Black September terrorist organization. (To this day, many athletes, coaches, and government officials blame German Olympic organizers for their lax security and inept response to the crisis.)

At the next summer games, in Montreal, East Germans dominated the gold medal count, especially in swimming, sweeping eleven out of a possible thirteen first-place finishes. For the athletes and their trainers and coaches, participating in the games offered a momentary glimpse of freedom, along with prestige. For Olympic officials who accompanied them, it offered the chance to avail themselves of goods they never even saw in East Germany. For the sixteen million people of this otherwise dismal and isolated communist state, winning medals brought international prominence.

The U.S. team's 1980 boycott of the Moscow Olympics provided another opportunity for the East Germans. Competing against Eastern Bloc countries, the GDR flourished with athletic successes while struggling to be recognized as a true power broker. East German athletes again dominated the Games, with not only gold but world records. Then, in 1984, the Russians, along with their Eastern allies, retaliated by boycotting the United States Games in Los Angeles. So, the cold war continued, both on and off the playing field. Meanwhile, East German scientists were hard at work preparing for the next chemically engineered Olympic Games.

All of this gold-medal success did not go unnoticed at IOC headquarters in Lausanne, Switzerland. There, IOC chairman Juan Antonio Samaranch, chief counsel François Carrard, and IOC medical chief Alexandre deMerode from Belgium were trying to balance the playing field. It was apparent that new doping protocols were being outsmarted by GDR doctors and pharmaceutical companies. While not wanting to be "soft" on doping and steroid use, which was known to be widespread, Samaranch was also concerned about the image of his five "magic rings" and the billion-dollar corporate sponsorships and television contracts. He knew that too many positive drug tests would have a severe impact on the public—that television viewers would turn their sets off in disgust, were it to become known that the true winners of sport were just performance-enhanced athletes.

Samaranch also had to keep his Eastern Bloc countries in check. In 1985, he flew to East Berlin and was welcomed by Manfred Ewald, the mastermind of GDR sports under President Erich Honecker. Samaranch and Ewald were close friends and colleagues. In fact, prior to their meeting, Samaranch had awarded Ewald the Olympic Order, a congressional medal type of honor, given only to those select officials who uphold the "perfect ideal of sport and humanity." Two other officials, East Germany's Honecker and Romanian dictator Nicolae Ceauşescu, were both awarded Gold Olympic Order awards for their contributions to sport and society. Overthrown in a popular uprising, Ceauceşcu and his wife, Elena, were swiftly executed on December 25, 1989, after a brief trial. Honecker was indicted for manslaughter in 1992, but in 1993 Germany chose not to make him stand trial. He slipped away to Chile, where he died in May 1994.

If only the scholar de Coubertin could return to Lausanne for one day, he might realize that his lofty ideal of keeping sport free of political agendas and extravagant power plays was the last thing the modern kings and queens of the Olympic movement had in mind.

5

The Franke Files

It is July of 1998, and I am about to have dinner at a Heidelberg restaurant with Professor Werner Franke, the person most responsible for exposing the documents proving not only that GDR athletes were illegally doped, but that there was a government plan for doing so. Now the foremost European expert on doping, he is the one who blew the whistle on the German sports monster machine.

Professor Franke and his wife arrive late. That is not unusual, since he is at the center of a media frenzy surrounding the trials. "Sorry again, but it was the French media," he says to me with a bit of sarcasm in his voice. Franke appears in the press almost daily, giving radio and TV interviews by the dozens. This time he had been cornered on the subject of a new doping scandal. Festina, the French team of the Tour de France cycling event, has just been busted for using a carload of anabolics, EPO (the blood-thickening agent that increases the flow of oxygen), and amphetamines—and, of course, masking agents so that no drug lab could detect the stuff.

After dinner, the plates are whisked away with typical German precision. We need to make room for some papers; not just any papers, but the STASI files, the written reports by the GDR's secret police. Some are original documents with black marks obscuring the names. Some are imprinted with red ink stamped with large seals, stating in German, "approved for release by the German prosecutor."

One of the documents mentions Dr. Dieter Binus. He is the only East German doctor on trial who has agreed to testify with full disclosure. Yes, he did give steroids to young women, not injections and not very high in dosage, but yes, he did do it. In exchange for his testimony, plus implicating others involved in doping, he will pay a small fine. This is the plea bargain that his defense team has worked out with the Berlin prosecutors. Other doctors have fled the country; some are now in China practicing a similar brand of human engineering on a new crop of youngsters. Those who stay in Germany may do jail time or may just be fined for their crimes against humanity.

Another document contains a name I recognize from many recent news stories, that of Dr. Helmut Riedel. "Dr. Riedel was being investigated by so many people," Franke says with a wide grin. "There was a state plan for everything in the East," he notes. "Yes, Riedel was the big steroid guy, and the secret police had a plan for him to keep him happy," he continues. "You see, everyone in East Germany was looking out for everyone else, while the master plan was in operation. The STASI had so many plans that it was mind-numbing. Who had time for sport when everyone was spying on the spies?" he muses.

How Professor Franke came into possession of these files makes for an interesting story in itself. Since the 1960s, when Franke was her coach, Brigitte Berendonk had told him that her East German competitors were using drugs for performance enhancement. Doping, she told him, was a common practice in the GDR. In 1989, after years of hearing anecdotal accounts of this widespread doping from Brigitte and others, Franke learned that there were classified documents somewhere outlining years of a state drug plan. Some of the files had been kept by the STASI. Their whereabouts became known to him from stories that had been leaked to the media. Later that year, at the time of the fall of the Berlin Wall and the beginning of reunification, Franke heard that many documents were being destroyed to protect former government officials. Indeed, many documents were destroyed, although some were collected by the Sports Medical Service, an arm of the government.

However, a set of documents was found at the medical academy of the National People's Army in Bad Saarow, east of Berlin. By obtaining a court order, Franke was able to locate and retrieve these military documents. There he found in detail the doping plan and athlete records as well as the implementation strategy. The plan clearly pointed to the training facility at Leipzig and the major drug lab at Kreischa.

In late 1990, Franke, as a member of the Academy of Sciences, was asked to evaluate some of the research institutes that had participated in doping practices. In the course of making his evaluation, he located a series of notebooks giving the exact times, dosages, and injection schedules of steroids administered to thousands of athletes over twenty-five years. Later that year came another turning point: Franke learned that Dr. Manfred Höppner, chief of sports medicine for all of the GDR, had just sold very sensitive Documents to *Stern* magazine. These documents provided an outline of the doping plan.

In 1994, Franke was given access to an archive of STASI files identifying prominent M.D.s and Ph.D.s who had collaborated with the government and the STASI to use performance-enhancement drugs. Soon after that, he met high-level people who had defected from the GDR and reported that some 150 archives, containing tens of thousands of pages documenting twenty-five years of doping, were located with the STASI. These documents also revealed for the first time that virilization and other deadly side effects were known to the doctors as far back as 1966.

Finally, in late 1994, the Bundestag published an official report outlining the GDR's master plan for doping its elite athletes. This report led to the 412 indictments by the Berlin prosecutors.

"They had a search warrant for me and they wanted the documents," Franke says, speaking of an incident that occurred in early 1991. "I saw the search warrant and I know the judge." Franke smiles ruefully, as if to say, this is a big game. Brigitte looks more serious though. She knows that although it is the 1990s, the German police still raid homes in the middle of the night. She understands that lives have been threatened and people have disappeared after they came forward to bear witness. Brigitte is concerned, too, that Werner never sleeps. Even now, she fears that something bad will happen to him and the rest of the story will not get out.

The conversation at the table turns to the awkward situation in which the athletes find themselves. "A triple jumper wrote to us and said he didn't want to take dope, so he chose not to," she says. "But the coach convinced him that he needed the drugs, so he had to take them. The athlete then convinced himself and felt justified because they coerced him. The pressure was enormous. This is very sad. It is so pathetic. And now we have the Tour de France with all the EPO, amphetamines, and steroids. It still goes on. . . . People make the argument that you can't compete without it. One has to learn to question; we as an institution have to learn from our mistakes," she says in dismay.

"It is only honorable to admit this fault," she contends. "So the victim now feels better about giving something back. My orthopedic doctor friend wanted to disclose the fact, but she was fearful about her future career, so she chose to keep quiet even though in her heart she knew it was wrong. To stand up in court is very difficult; it is so painful," she says.

Brigitte is becoming more animated. "Now the doctors are denigrating the athletes who are testifying. They call them fat pigs and out of shape and not of the highest quality. It is very difficult to bear witness. The GDR lives on in many devious ways," she says, nodding.

"An Olympic canoer called me. Her mother is a relative of mine by marriage. There was a reunion of our family and she said to this relative why not talk about the steroid use. She had kept a journal secretly. She had kept track of her daily 'vitamin' intake, a lovely euphemism for doping. She said that the top athletes don't want to talk; they want to maintain their anonymous status. But my relative had serious menstruation problems in the late 1980s after competition, which led to excessive bleeding and very serious gynecological disorders. And so the dilemma goes! These athletes had their moments of glory, they cherished those moments, their benefits, their cars, their expense accounts, so now they don't want to turn against the system," she explains. "Some are willing to live with the hurt, the pain, perhaps out of guilt. Who knows for sure?"

Brigitte looks as if she were searching for some meaning. "The medals are great legacies to show my grandchildren; the moment of glory is still and will always be there, regardless of the drugs," she says. "But it is a higher honor to come forward to tell the truth. This is a true moment of glory." Her eyes are bright with passion. Then a look of frustration crosses her face. "We need to return to normal and to human competition; so maybe it takes a bit longer to run the race or throw the discus, but we need to go back to real competition. We slow it down a bit. Why not change the system and turn back the clock?" she says.

Later, Brigitte turns philosophical after her husband leaves with their son Ulrich for another media interview. Franke is constantly in motion, perhaps out of fear or perhaps because of a sense of destiny. "The bird that has defiled the nest," she sighs. "This is a bad thing for us former GDR athletes. When we tell the truth, we are defiling our nation, the image of our greatness and our prestige. We feel that we must defend ourselves and our heritage and be courageous by standing up in court. It is a terrible dilemma to go to court and be exposed. In everyday life, we are being punished on the one hand and then praised for standing up. It is a paradoxical situation, and very tough."

It is late. We begin to walk in the night air. "We are now in a new stage of victimization," she says with a hint of despair. "Werner and I are no longer members of the sports community. We are somewhat independent of this, so we can be a bit detached. But it is hard." Brigitte looks as if she is seeking affirmation. "There is this pool where I swim as a fish, and I must ask myself every day, how can I pollute the water that I swim in? This is the metaphor by which we must live."

"Some athletes are still in hiding," she continues, "because they fear the loss of status and prestige in the athletic family. Others can stand aside and speak the truth. It is a decision of personal integrity; we must learn to teach our children about integrity. I wonder what will happen to the athletes who have to give up their medals, their identity, their self-esteem. Andreas Krieger, who used be known as Hormone Heidi [before he went through a sex change] wants to return the medal. He [formerly she] won the gold. He wants to give the medal to someone; he doesn't feel worthy of keeping it. But how to do this?" Brigitte wonders. "Werner advises Krieger to offer the medal to the German sports teachers as an honor to promote healthy sport in youth. We don't know how it will play out.

"And then there is the volleyball athlete who wrote to us," she says, continuing with her list of victims. "She talked about her operations and her gynecological complications, but then she vanished; we were unable to contact her after the first letter. Her phone was disconnected, she moved. And this has happened many times. People read about our court case, they called, they wrote, and they wanted to share their feelings, but then they disappeared," she says.

"You know, the women would not shower together. They had to shave all over their bodies to remove the excess hair; they were embarrassed about being naked. So they would call us and tell us these horror stories, but then they would disappear."

Brigitte offers another story. "A hammer thrower whom I know was put on lots of steroids and fell into a deep coma and then went into a psychiatric hospital. He wanted to keep his illness a secret. He survived the ordeal and now works in a butcher shop.

"This UM stuff, the 'supporting means,' was a clever disguise, the ultimate deceit, the *1984* George Orwell Newspeak," she says sardonically. "But this was the Deutsche Republik, the great GDR. I had to go to court already to defend myself. I was sued by a Frenchman and had to go to Paris for the trial. I lost the case, and the judge made me pay a token of one franc for the libel and defamation," she says with a bittersweet smile. "Of course, I had to pay for my lawyer, and that was very expensive: thirty thousand DM. But the judge felt that I did not really defame, so it was a loss but a token loss, perhaps a winning outcome.

"And so you come to terms with the situation," she says wearily. "In German we call that *'Alfabisen'*; it is the scar and then the wound, and it heals and then you don't want to reopen the wound. And so, suing your doctor or coach, it is a betrayal, and it is so painful to reopen that.

"It is hard to have it both ways," she admits; "the benefits, the medals, the records; and now to turn against these people. The doctors also suffered as they were working for the STASI, the secret police. They reported the abuses, but the STASI forced them to continue. Everyone was part of the scheme; it was an institutional scheme. There were penalties for doctors and anyone who turned against them. 'If I didn't do it, someone else would have done it.' " She looks at me as if she thinks I have read this story somewhere before. "It is wrong to dope. Yet on the other hand, we have our coaches and our friends and they looked after us . . . so it is a dilemma. You don't want to contaminate all that they did for you."

6

Modern Drugs for a Modern Olympics

The coaches and doctors of the GDR did do a lot for the athletes in their elite training program, watching over their development and progress with considerable care. If they provided their charges with "something extra," it could be argued that they were acting in the interest of furthering the sport. But I knew, as did others who worked in the field of high-level sports, that the substances administered to the East German athletes could not be used without serious medical consequences. Just what was so terrible about these drugs, and how does performance enhancement work? To comprehend fully the gravity of their use, I turned to Professor Werner Franke for an explanation of the pharmacology of the drugs in question.

Dr. Franke first talked about the normal functions of the male hormones. "The male sexual hormones, androgens, to which testosterone and its derivatives as anabolic steroids belong, are required by both sexes for their entire life span, from the various sexual differentiations of the embryo to the development of sexual characteristics during puberty," he explained. "They are also necessary for the maintenance of sexual functions and for reproduction. Besides these sexually specific properties, androgens are used in the generation of new cells and structures for the skeletal muscles, and for bone and fat formation, as well as for organs such as the brain, the prostate, and the kidneys. These extremely variant biological effects are signaled by special androgen receptors in the cells. By means of these receptors, the androgen forms a complex that moves into the kernel of the cell, and there provides special information to the genetic material (DNA). The cell reacts to this by building new proteins."

As Franke explained further, the biologically active androgen is primarily found in the testicles, the ovaries, the adrenal glands, the skin, and the fatty tissues. Men produce between 2.5 mg and 10 mg of testosterone daily, while women produce only about one-tenth of that. The plasma level of testosterone for men correspondingly runs to about 3,000 to 9,000 pg/ml, where for women the figure is only 100 to 500 pg/ml.

"The use of 'supportive means' in the GDR was an excuse to build a major performance-enhancement athletic machine," Professor Franke said. "Supportive means," or UM as it was commonly referred to, were substances produced by VEB Jenapharm, mainly consisting of Oral-Turinabol and their derivatives. These tablets contained chlordehydromethyltestosterone as the active ingredient, dispensed to athletes in 1 mg (small pink tablets) and 5 mg (small blue tablets) form.

As Franke explained, other products included the Turinabol ampule preparations, and Turinabol-Depot ampules, which were used in intramuscular injections. Turinabol ampules contained nandrolone phenyl propionate as the active agent, to 25 mg in a 1 ml viscous solution, and Turinabol-Depot ampules contained nandrolone decanoate as the active agent, to 50 mg in a 1 ml viscous solution. Oral-Turinabol tablets, as well as Turinabol ampules and Turinabol-Depot ampules, are anabolic steroids. "It's that simple," Franke said. To differentiate them from testosterone, they are designated as testosterone derivatives. The ingestion or use of these anabolic preparations can be verified by urine testing within a specific time period after ingestion, because the metabolites of these preparations can be clearly identified in the urine, thereby providing evidence of the medication.

After 1978, Turinabol-Depot ampules were no longer used in the GDR's program. It had been determined by this point that their metabolites remained in the body for too long, and for that reason they could no longer be used in the immediate precompetition preparations, posing a serious problem for GDR sports doctors.

In their place, the intramuscular injections of choice were Testosterone-Depot and the widely used preparation of testosterone ampules, which contained 25 mg of testosterone-propionate. This preparation of testosterone ampules was advantageous for athletes because it could not be differentiated from the body's own naturally occurring testosterone.

"In the early drug-testing days of the late 1970s, Oral-Turinabol and other testosterone derivatives could not be detected by simple urinalysis," Franke said. "Without the proper testing of testosterone, its use in top athletics remained possible. From 1978 to around 1981, the GDR continued its testosterone programs in top-level athletics in the immediate precompetition preparations.

But things changed dramatically in 1981 when a prominent pharmacologist in Cologne, Professor Manfred Donike, developed an indirect procedure to test for testosterone, in which the relationship between testosterone and epitestosterone in the body of an athlete could be measured. "He was a brilliant scientist and was well respected by all of our colleagues," Franke said. Donike understood that the natural quotient in our bodies should provide readings at a level of 2. The introduction of external testosterone would, of course, lead to higher readings. Any reading higher than 2 would lead to the conclusion that "outside" testosterone had been introduced into the body. Dr. Donike discussed the idea with the IOC Medical Commission (he formed the first committee within the Olympic movement) and designed the international standard for acceptable levels of body testosterone. Today, the ratio of 6:1 is still the standard that is accepted; that is, if the quotient of testosterone to epitestosterone were to read higher than 6 to 1, you would be considered "over the limit" and disqualified from competition. Over the past twenty years, many great athletes have lost gold medals because of this test and the infamous testosterone ratio.

The GDR exploited the 6:1 ratio and, through their own brilliant scientists, found a way to beat the system again. Back at their lab, they began to manufacture artificial epitestosterone. Now they could continue to administer testosterone, but could also administer countering dosages of epitestosterone for security against doping tests and possible Olympic sanctions. By giving their athletes both hormones, the testosterone and epitestosterone, they could enable them to maintain the delicate 6:1 balance and pass the required urine tests.

Franke explained that the use of anabolic steroids in tablet form as well as in injections came about in this way: The half-life of testosterone, and therefore the time required to purge it from the body, is short, ranging from ten to twenty minutes. That means that testosterone taken orally is quickly cleansed from the body by the action of the liver. The most productive form of the hormone is the testosterone-ester (fat + acid conjunctions of testosterone) in a viscous solution injected directly into the muscle.

Franke noted that other doping preparations were used in GDR top-level swimming. Among these was the STS 646, another synthetic hormone, also known as mestanolone and also produced by VEB Jenapharm. But STS 646 was dangerous and therefore unlicensed in the GDR. It was occasionally used alongside the classic anabolic, Oral-Turinabol, to stimulate testosterone production. Other drugs used during the heyday of GDR doping were gonabion ampules, also known as hCG and clomiphen, as well as neuropeptides in the form of the preparation oxytocin, which was designated by the code name "B 17." In 1977, the pervitin series (also known as speed tabs) was brought into use in GDR swimming as well.

From German science to German performance, it all seemed to work like a BMW road test. With the pills and injections, athletes did achieve the Olympic motto of: *Citius, Altius, Fortius* (Swifter, Higher, and Stronger)." The effects of the anabolics did increase muscle development and shorten recovery time. The outcomes were achieved with German precision, but the long-term risks of steroid use were high.

The GDR doctors knew all of this, as they had ongoing contact with the scientists at Jenapharm. In effect, they were not only sports-medicine experts but also pioneers in DNA engineering.

Speaking of the deadly side effects of anabolic steroids, Franke said that he knew what his colleagues in the GDR knew, which was, quite simply, that anabolics in men and in women can lead to a transitory elevation in the transaminasen SGOT and SGPT. These are clear indicators of the destruction of liver cells, resulting in peliosis hepatitis and leading to liver tumors and terminal liver cancer. Multiple cases of heart attacks have also been attributed to androgen use among athletes. And, as we all know, many U.S. athletes have succumbed to heart failure.

The GDR brain trust also knew that women were more vulnerable when using anabolic steroids. On the one hand, their performances could be spectacular: greater, in fact, than that of the men, but the risks were a lot higher. Typical side effects resulting from administering these hormones to women include retarded growth, disturbances in fertility, and heart disease. Other problems include deepening of the voice (mostly an irreversible situation), an increase in body hair on the legs, pubic hair extending to the navel and beyond, and, more dangerously, the enlargement of the clitoris (clitoris-hypertrophy). Beyond that, the scientists knew early on that testosterone derivatives such as Oral-Turinabol or Turinabol-Depot ampules disturb the so-called releasing hormone in the hypothalamus, which controls the pulse generator.

As a result of disrupting the pulse generator, the control

hormones LH and FSH, which are formed in the hypophysis, and which control the ovulation cycle, are disrupted. Beyond that, anabolic-androgen steroids affect the lipids in the blood, meaning they influence the fat metabolism. Regular, recurring use lowers so-called "good" or nominal HDL cholesterol, and elevates the so-called "bad" or damaging LDL cholesterol.

Franke stated emphatically that the risks and side effects of anabolic steroids administered to women and young girls were absolutely well-known to the trainers and doctors in GDR women's swimming. In spite of this knowledge, the doctors and trainers continued dispensing drugs because they believed that without the use of anabolic steroids there would be no medals or successes in international competitions. They also recognized that athletic successes were a prerequisite for financial bonuses, promotions, awards, and other preferential treatment in the GDR system. And, as Brigitte Berendonk had emphasized, without that preferential treatment, the progress of one's life in that system would come to a stop.

7

The Bad Saarow Trip

While they essentially knew what had been going in East Germany's elite sports training program, Brigitte Berendonk and Werner Franke had long been frustrated in their quest for evidence. Before the fall of the Wall, they had heard through underground sources in East Germany that Dr. Helmut Riedel, an influential GDR sports official, had brazenly written his Ph.D. dissertation on the use of Oral-Turinabol in the decades-long "supportive measures" campaign. But they were warned that the Riedel work ("Dissertation B") had been destroyed, together with other secret STASI-controlled sports records, just before reunification.

In 1991, however, Berendonk and Franke received critical information on a surviving secret archive of documents on the East German doping apparatus, material that had been too sensitive for all but high-clearance STASI officers to assemble in one collection. Dr. Riedel's elusive dissertation was said to be in these archives, which were located at the former GDR military hospital in Bad Saarow, a suburb of the former East Berlin. In recognition of their decades of tireless research, the couple received permission from the government to examine the documents.

What they uncovered was both a shock and a personal vindication of their crusade. Beyond the Riedel dissertation, they saw an exhaustive ten-volume classified archive that documented every East German athletic event of the previous three decades, each denoted by an asterisk with an athlete's name and a performance-enhancing chemical, along with his or her ranking in the competition. Berendonk and Franke had discovered a virtually invaluable treasure: proof that would change the history not only of Olympic and international competitive sport, but also that of East Germany's soulless political system, which had consumed its own most promising youth in a ruthless attempt to achieve glory.

The centerpiece of this archive was "State Planning Theme 14.25," a meticulously organized project, begun in the 1950s, designed to elevate the GDR's international prestige through the athletic prowess of its Olympic and national teams.

For Berendonk and Franke, the Riedel dissertation and State Planning Theme 14.25 comprised the Rosetta Stone for solving the mystery with which they had been struggling for so long. In full, damning detail, the documents provided a blueprint for the astounding accomplishments of East Germany's athletes, but also for the basis of their apparent invincibility in the face of high-technology drug testing.

According to these documents, the GDR's performance-enhancement plan rested on the use of anabolic steroids, synthetic compounds similar to natural hormones. As Franke confirmed in our discussions, it had long been known that steroids could be used to enhance performance by adding muscle mass and increasing endurance. During World War II, Hitler issued vast quantities of steroids to the SS and the Wehrmacht so that his troops would better resist combat fatigue and be more ruthless in following any order. As early as 1941, Soviet Red Army observers had noted an unusually passionate fighting spirit among German soldiers, who often seemed eager to die for the glory of the Third Reich.

The leaders of the GDR's sports machine built on scientific knowledge gleaned in the Nazi era to carry this human engineering experiment a giant step forward. Their program had a single goal: to transform the German Democratic Republic from a lackluster Soviet satellite into a giant in the global arena of competitive sport. Within this context, the quadrennial Olympic Games were the summit of ambition, and the maximum, in effort and financial resources, was dedicated toward amassing Olympic medals.

The Bad Saarow archive records clearly established that the synthetic steroid Oral-Turinabol enabled young athletes to build muscle mass with dramatic speed, in transformations of body type that almost rivalled the "morphing" in today's science-fiction dramas. The East German researchers had also found that their anabolic steroids seemed to reverse the negative effects of exercise. Instead of muscle tissue breaking down, as it normally does during prolonged exercise, the muscles of the athletes on steroids grew stronger and resisted the strains and tears that plague most rigorous, extended workout routines.

Within months of the first dosages of the "supportive measures" in the 1950s, East German athletes had embarked on the superhuman workout programs that became the hallmark of their national sports effort.

But the researchers had also quickly discovered that the drugs affected the mind as well as the body. Sometime after taking these drugs, the athletes—like the shock troops of Hitler's elite SS units—reported a sense of invincibility, unlimited energy, and an uncontrollable libido. Early in the program, female athletes as young as fourteen embarked on sexual rampages in the sports complexes, which their trainers, coaches, and physicians ignored as long as the girls performed well in the pool or on the track.

Less than a year into the project, sports organization physicians and trainers were documenting serious and sometimes life-threatening physiological changes in the young athletes. These included debilitating liver complaints, disrupted menstrual cycles, enlargement of genitalia in young females (but atrophy in that of boys), irregular heart rhythms, and hazardous imbalances of serum-cholesterol levels. Yet no promising athlete was ever removed from the drug regimen because of health risks.

The researchers eventually established what they described as "safe" rotating three-and-four-week training cycles, during which Oral-Turinabol was administered daily in pink 1 mg or blue 5 mg tablets. Depending on the athletes' potential for success and membership in a prestigious event cadre (such as the women's swimming and track and field teams), they might receive as many as six of these intense drug-and-training workups in a twelve-month period.

After the Munich Olympics, there was widespread speculation and, later, confirmed reports of prolific steroid use at the Games. This led to the IOC's new and revised protocols for drug testing and a complete ban on all anabolic steroids. New high-tech drug-testing equipment was made available to the most advanced labs in the world in order to screen for illegal substances. In order to thwart the increasingly reliable drug-detection mechanism involving both gas chromatography and mass-spectrometer urinalysis that gradually came into use following the 1974 ban on anabolic steroids, GDR sports officials developed a complex and effective defense. Generally, the researchers discovered, all detectable traces of Oral-Turinabol disappeared from the body ten days after the last dose. But to be certain of success, up to five potential individual medalists were selected and trained for every event. They were put through slightly staggered drug-enhanced training regimens. Then the use of drugs tapered off, to end ten days before the scheduled international or Olympic event.

This cynical manipulation of young athletes' lives continued throughout the glory years of East German sport. Not until the lifting of the Iron Curtain in 1989 was the international athletic community able to institute mandatory random drug testing in training camps such as SC Dynamo in East Berlin. By then the damage had been done and the East had collapsed.

During its heyday, however, the East German doping machine was virtually unassailable. But as the program rapidly expanded in the 1960s, it became vital to maintain its secret nature. For this reason, the STASI quickly assumed a central role as the tacit administrator and shadow facilitator of the "supportive measures" system. Although this move did ensure secrecy, at the same time, the STASI's compulsive record-keeping also ensured that the damning evidence would be preserved.

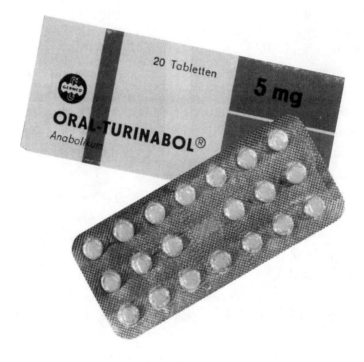

Oral-Turinabol, a testosterone derivative, was produced by VEB Jenapharm lab in Germany and was the drug of choice for most doping doctors during the GDR heyday.

DDR-Doping: Organization and Distribution
From the Mid-1960s until 1989

State Office for Physical Development and Sports

STATE SECRETARIES
Alfred B. Neumann (until 1968)
Roland Weissig (1968–1974)
Professor Dr. Günter Erbach (1974–1989)
DIRECTOR SINCE 1965

SUPERVISION AND IMPLEMENTATION

Central Committee of the SED

SECRETARIES RESPONSIBLE FOR SPORT
Erich Honecker (until 1971)
Paul Verner (1971–1983)
Egon Krenz (1983–1989)
WORKING TOGETHER WITH THE DIRECTOR OF THE SPORTS DIVISION IN THE CENTRAL COMMITTEE
Rudolf Hellmann

DIRECTION AND CONTROL

Manfred Ewald [since 1988: Klaus Eichler]

GERMAN SPORTS FEDERATION ("DTSB") PRESIDENT, MEMBER OF THE CENTRAL COMMITTEE OF THE SED

Manfred Ewald (German Sports Federation—DTSB); Dr. Manfred Höppner (Sports Medical Service—SMD); Professor Dr. Alfons Lehnert (FKS). These individuals are responsible for determining the supporting substance guidelines for a four year period and approving the application concepts for the various Sports Federations in the German Sports Federation (DTSB) in one year intervals for all sports clubs. Acquisition and financing of doping substances occurs through the State Secretary's office, the Sports Medical Service (SMD) and the High Achievement Sports Federation (LSK) of the DDR.

ASK and SVD are able, through their own pharmacies, to obtain additional doping substances without approval from the German Sports Federation (DTSB) and the Sports Medical Service (SMD).

RESPONSIBILITY AND DECISION MAKING IN ALL DOP!NG QUESTIONS

Dr. Manfred Höppner [SMD]. Professor Dr. Alfons Lehnert [FKS]. Federation Doctors. Federation Trainers

Determine every four years the supporting substance guidelines and make an annual determination of the appropriate applications for the Sports Federations in the German Sports Federation (DTSB).

Dr. Manfred Höppner [SMD]. Doping Control Laboratory Kreischa

Testing of all athletes prior to departure for competition in another country. In the event of a positive result, provide information to the DTSB.

Professor Dr. Edelfrid Buggel [SKS] Professor Dr. Alfons Lehnert [FKS]. Dr. Rolf Donath [ZI]

Research for doping substances as well as the prevention of side effects.

Professor Dr. Edelfrid Buggel [SKS]. Academy of Research. Director

Doping research and production of non-medically indicated substances with proven doping effect.

Dr. Manfred Höppner [SMD]

and his co-workers in Berlin direct a courier of the Sports Medical Service (SMD) to deliver the substances. Frequently, the appropriate Federation doctor picks the doping substances personally, to distribute them according to the central directive. The courier transports substances and the list of names with applicable dosages to the fifteen federations. At that point, the Division Director for High Achievement Sport takes the supporting substances and the accompanying documents. He gives these, in exchange for a receipt, to the Division Doctor for the applicable sports club. This doctor destroys the original packaging. He counts the pills and packs them in an unlabeled envelope and gives them to the trainer. The trainer and the Division Doctor determine the individual dose for each athlete.

Athletes

as a general rule were required to take the supporting substances in the presence of the trainer. Injections of anabolic substances were adminstered by the Division Doctor. The athletes do not receive an explanation regarding the purpose, risks, and side effects of the supporting substances. In certain unavoidable situations, athletes are told either the complete or partial truth, and are then required to sign a Confidentiality Agreement.

APPRECIATION IS EXTENDED TO GISELHER SPITZER FOR USE OF THIS TABLE

8

Shit Hits the Fan

Although Werner Franke and his wife, Brigitte, had spoken out for years about the widespread use of illegal drugs, it wasn't until 1997 that the dam broke. Franke went public with his discoveries of several papers, including an academic journal article that laid the groundwork for the Bundestag to unleash sixty-one Berlin prosecutors and file 412 indictments against the perpetrators of the German doping machine.

Franke knew the stories; he had met hundreds of athletes who had been doped. Now he had the proof. His source was the series of meticulously written documents, which had been classified and held in deep vaults of the secret archives of the Ministry for State Security. By 1989, when unification was under way and some of the information about the secret doping plan had leaked to the press, there was a mad scramble to collect all documents and shred them. But Franke now had the last remaining copy from Bad Saarow. As he expected, the documents revealed that over some thirty years, major human experimentation on world-class athletes had been carried out at the Research Institute for Physical Culture and Sports in Leipzig. Some work had been performed at the central doping control lab (Zentrales Dopinkontrollabor) in Kreischa under the direction of deputy director and chief physician of GDR doping, Dr. Manfred Höppner.

These documents had been well hidden and available only to STASI police officials, but an act of greed and stupidity offered an extraordinary opportunity to Professor Franke in early 1990. Manfred Höppner, in an act of desperation and, perhaps, ego gratification, had sold sealed documents from the STASI files to the weekly German magazine *Stern* for a handsome profit. *Stern* noted that some STASI files covered thirty years and contained more than 10,000 pages of evidence. It was the most comprehensive and massive doping scheme anywhere in the world.

According to these documents, the main training "vitamin" and source of all GDR athletic pride was the androgenic-anabolic steroid known as Oral-Turinabol. The performance results were stunning, with dramatic increases in discus, hammer, and shot-put by leaps and bounds after just 20 mg of the small pink tablets over eleven weeks. It was the miracle training drug, producing scores of winners and unbelievable athletic feats. However, the little pills had some negative effects: young girls emerged at the 1976 Olympic games looking like NFL linebackers, with gruff voices, huge shoulders, and hair growing in very odd places. The GDR women swept the gold-medal count in Montreal, winning eleven out of thirteen events, and leaving the Americans and Canadians in the dust. Höppner reported in bold type the dramatic impact of his doping experiment when he wrote to the STASI headquarters on March 3,

1977: "Anabolics are used in all Olympic sports and the effects of the performances are undoubted. Remarkable rates of performance enhancement with women swimmers, this is where our greatest strength and advantages are."

What Werner Franke had stumbled on was more than he had ever imagined. The documents Höppner had sold to *Stern* had broader implications than he had anticipated.

The directive to achieve international dominance in athletics had come from the Politburo of the Socialist Unity Party (SED) of the GDR, which was the highest level of decision-making in the government, and therefore also the highest power apparatus of the GDR at that time. Manfred Ewald, who had been president of the Deutsche Turn and Sportbund (DTSB) until 1988, was the liaison to the Central Committee of the SED, and as such, was the individual responsible for implementing the directive. Ewald was himself a member of the Central Committee of the SED. In other words, the entire system was set up as an arm of the government: a vehicle for the GDR to gain international recognition through sports dominance.

Another major figure, Rudolf Hellmann, was the director of the sports department within the Central Committee of the SED. His deputy director was Walter Gröger. The Leistungssportkommission (LSK), under the chairmanship of Manfred Ewald, served as the connecting component between the SED and the athletic sports and research organizations. Other members of the LSK, in addition to Manfred Ewald, included the vice president of the DTSB, a Professor Röder, a representative of the Forschungsinstitut für Körperkultur und Sport (FKS), who also served as the current director of the sports department in the Central Committee of the SED. The LSK was responsible for policy decisions, which could then be implemented in detail by the remaining organizational structures of the GDR. All of this infrastructure was in place to win medals and thereby prove the superiority of the East.

The infrastructure of the GDR doping machine was the ultimate driving mechanism of their gold-medal success. The DTSB operated as an umbrella organization over all athletic associations in the GDR. It was composed of fifteen Bezirk (district) athletic organizations throughout East Germany, in which the city, county, and regional athletic organizations, sports associations, and the district committees of the athletic associations were included. The DeutscherSchwimmsport-Verband (DSSV) was also a member of the DTSB, under DSSV president Georg Zorowka. The association was focused on skill development in the GDR and on the establishment of so-called cadre groups— national or Olympic Team cadres. Their singular focus was to win lots of medals.

Reviewing more of the documents, Franke learned that every athletic association had an association doctor. The association doctor for DSSV was Dr. Lothar Kipke. He had the responsibility for all medical problems attributed to the training; he supervised the preparation for competitions and monitored any medicinal needs at the site of the competition. The association doctor also chaired the Doctor's Commission of the DSSV, which included oversight of the swimming section of Sport Club SC Dynamo Berlin.

As the association doctor for DSSV, Dr. Kipke also had the honor of being a collaborator with the STASI police, reporting to them regularly under the code name "Rolf." Franke had suspicions all along, but now he had evidence that virtually all senior sports officials, including the infamous "Rolf," were neatly tied to the STASI secret police.

Franke also learned from the *Stern* article that the Staatssekretariat für Körperkultur und Sport (SKS), or State Secretariat for Physical Culture and Sport, was an important component relative to the goals and interests of all GDR sports. The SKS had been created as an independent operating agency in 1970 as a state organ of the Council of Ministers of the GDR. The SKS took the tasks and functions of a "Ministry of Sport for the GDR" seriously, in that it assumed responsibility for the planning and management of all state activities. Along with the planning of athletic facilities, equipment, and materials, the SKS was also responsible for the development and direction of sport science and for the education of trainers and instructors at the Deutsche Hochschule für Körperkultur (German Academy for Physical Culture) in Leipzig.

The SKS was directly subordinate to the Sports Medicine Service (SMD) of the GDR and the Research Institute for Physical Culture and Sport in Leipzig (FKS), which was affiliated with the German Academy. The SMD in turn was subordinate to the Central Institute (ZI) of the Sports Medicine Service in the town of Kreischa. A doping control laboratory in Kreischa served as an important unit of the ZI, as it was the key to beating future International Olympic Committee doping tests.

All of these organizations supported each other in their common goal of achieving significant numbers of Olympic medals. This was to be accomplished by exploiting the advances made in research and science, as well as through trainer education. This goal was furthered by optimizing the preparation process before competitions, and of course, by having the unconditional medical support of the best doping doctors in the modern world.

The Deutsche Hochschule für Körperkultur and the FKS

were responsible for all scientific research. Founded in 1950, the DHFK became the most important training site for all athletics within the GDR. Franke soon learned that this was the place where it had all begun. Trainers completing a regularized eight-semester program of education were awarded a diploma in athletic instruction. This is where coaches studied athletic recruiting, building state-of-the-art programs to secure the best and the biggest bodies for the GDR sports machine.

The Forschungsinstitut für Körperkultur und Sport (FKS) was housed on the grounds of the DHFK in Leipzig, where it was made into an independent scientific lab in 1969. Sports-medicine evaluations were conducted there, as well as improvisations in athletic-equipment construction. One of the best-known sports-medicine components in Leipzig was the Streaming Channel or "swimming canal," in which male and female swimmers of the GDR were tested annually within the context of "complex performance diagnostics." The swimmers were occasionally videotaped during these tests, and experimentation was conducted with respect to water-flow conditions while swimming. The ABC news magazine *Nightline* flew to Germany to tape footage of this equipment for a network showing in late 1998.

The sports-medicine service, with its specialized laboratories, was a part of the FKS. This is where newly developed pharmaceutical products were examined and evaluated to determine their suitability for enhancing the performance of high-level athletes. The results and findings of this research were secretly transmitted to the SMD.

The DHFK also profited from this research activity within the FKS, because the most recent findings from sports medicine and sports methodology could also be incorporated into the instruction materials for trainers and athletic instructors.

The head of this entire sports apparatus was Dr. Manfred Höppner. Franke and Berendonk were beginning to understand the depth of his role in the GDR sports world. Dr. Höppner was known throughout the scientific community as a clever and well-informed scientist, and of course, was a spy for the STASI as well. His undercover reporting occurred on a regular basis. He was known to certain high-level officials as "Technik."

The Key to the Gold!

Probably the most important piece of the GDR puzzle, also disclosed in the *Stern* article, was that of the drug lab and its advanced technology. The material Manfred Höppner documented, both in the *Stern* article and in the Bad Saarow archives, served as a guide for Franke, revealing the locations of other documents of the GDR's doping program, including doctoral dissertations, which gave more proof to the pervasive master plan. Some of the following details gave Franke a clear view of the doping protocols.

The key to GDR dominance—and gold-medal success and longevity—was the doping control laboratory in Kreischa. Built in 1977, this brain trust served to secure and to cover up the use of all performance-enhancing medications. The director of the laboratory, Dr. Claus Clausnitzer, also reported to the GDR authorities—and, like his other sports-medicine colleagues, used his code name—"Meschke"—when he checked in with headquarters.

Manfred Ewald was chairman of the LSK, president of the DTSB, and a member of the Central Committee of the

Socialist Unity Party (SED) of the GDR. He took on many roles, and, as a result, orchestrated the most decisive political organization of the GDR. As director of the two most prestigious sports organizations, he implemented the mission statement regarding high-performance athletics in the GDR.

One of the most successful and therefore most significant sport clubs in the GDR was the Sport Club SC Dynamo Berlin, where two prominent people—and police informers—Dr. Dieter Binus and trainer Rolf Gläser worked. The Ministry of the Interior of the GDR was the umbrella organization for SC Dynamo Club, which is why all employees, including the doctors, were members of the secret police. They all had their rank, service mandates, and special code names.

Dr. Binus had primary responsibility for the maintenance and care of all athletes at the club. He also decided when a medical specialist was needed for consultation and ensured that all female teams had a gynecologist available.

The system for discovery and development of suitable recruits for women's swimming was especially well organized at Sport Club SC Dynamo Berlin. Many young girls learned swimming at an early age either in the school system or at specialized training centers like the Berlin-Adlershof Club. The SC Dynamo Berlin sought out female swimmers whose physical build and motor skills or other talents made them especially suited for swimming. Recruitment began when girls were approximately eleven years of age, because entry into the Child and Youth Sport School (KJS) "Werner Seelenbinder" in the Schönhausen district of Berlin typically began at the fifth-grade level. Once chosen, suitable candidates were then sent to the Seelenbinder school. From a sports perspective, when a girl was accepted into the prestigious Seelenbinder, she automatically became a member of the Sport Club SC Dynamo Berlin. There, the big-time training began—as this is where athletes were under control of the all-powerful GDR sports machine and its top-secret doping regimens.

According to club training plans, each female swimmer was assigned an individualized swim schedule which contained individual stress ratings. These ratings were compared to the results achieved in training, to identify root causes of poorer performance, and to filter out problems. Lactate values were read on a regular basis by taking blood from the earlobe. These values allowed assessment of the conditioning level of the swimmers. On the basis of these values, and of observation of the training performance, it was possible to make individual decisions as to whether to order more intense workouts. From this assessment, coaches could then decide which athletes were ready for high-level competition.

If the swimmers were in Berlin, their training day typically began with in-water training, followed by classroom training, and then another in-water training period or workout-room activity. After lunch, another classroom training session followed, then back to the pool. This rigorous schedule went Monday through Friday, while Saturday generally consisted of only two training sessions. Sunday was a rest day. Swimmers whose parents lived in Berlin were able to live at home, while the swimmers from outlying areas were quartered at the Seelenbinder.

During an in-water training session in the buildup phase, in which physical conditioning was the objective, very long distances were assigned. Swimmers had to swim 8 km in the morning, followed by a session in the afternoon, for a total daily workout of 16 km. In the weight room, there was also no slack. Young women were pushed to their limits, stressing their arms and shoulders to the maximum.

During advance training camps, schoolwork and academic studies were interrupted so that athletes could push themselves to three training sessions daily. Some training camps were set up at Lindow, near Berlin, in Kienbaum, and on the Rabenberg Mountain. Additionally, some training took place in special high-altitude areas to enhance oxygen levels. Typically, this specialized training occurred four times annually, usually during the winter months. Swimmers would travel to Belmeken, Bulgaria, but in later years they would go to Mexico City, where they would train at 8,000 feet.

Significant training demands led to the belief by many sports-medicine professionals that swimmers needed to restore and to rebuild their bodies. Enter the brilliance of GDR science and pharmaceutical magic. Vitamins were provided in powdered form known as Dynvital, as well as in tablets. Specifically, this included vitamin C, vitamin B, vitamin E, vitamin B-6, and "Sumavit Forte." In addition, there were magnesium, iron, and egg-white preparations. These vitamins and minerals were given to the swimmers as a drink in the form of a tea or blended shake, or as a handful of tablets, which were set out by the trainers at the pool. Most athletes enjoyed their cocktail after a hearty workout, unaware that this was just the first phase of a multilevel pharmaceutical buildup.

Medicinal support also included electromyostimulation, glucose injections, and injections with alpha-lipoacids. Twice a year, a routine physical examination was conducted, to determine the health and condition of the swimmers. These physical examinations, usually performed by the section doctor, included blood work.

GDR sports-medicine experts left no stone unturned. They wanted complete control and dominance over every aspect of their athletes' lives. The doctors and trainers were interested in finding out as early as possible when their young female swimmers first began menstruation. This information could enable them to understand and control the hormonal processes related to menstruation, causing variance in performance and in the mood of the swimmer, which could become problematic, especially at competitions. Sometimes the trainers would ask the swimmers about their menstruation, and at other times the swimmers would voluntarily provide this information to their doctors. Because birth-control pills can achieve a smooth regulation of the menstrual cycle, female swimmers were told they had to swallow the pills. Sport Club SC Dynamo Berlin had a full-time gynecologist on staff, so young women were also given regular gynecological examinations.

Thus, every training variable, according to the records, was controlled by the doctors. With complete command over every area of their athletes' existence, optimum performance would be achieved at any cost.

10

The Oath of Irony

Obviously, the maintenance of secrecy was of paramount importance to the GDR doping program. Without the wholehearted participation of its trainers—those who were closest to the young athletes—the plan could not have proceeded. The details of how those trainers were brought into the picture had actually been divulged sometime before the bulk of the STASI documents came to light.

At one time, Michael Regner was one of the preeminent trainers in the swimming world. The trainer for swimming sensation Michael Gross and other German athletes, Regner had worked in Havelberg with the swim club ASK-Potsdam, where he became known as the king of "Ausschulungskandidaten," or motivation. In November 1990, he made a dramatic confession. He talked at length with the German magazine *Der Spiegel*.

The GDR athletes he worked with were gifted, but he gave them the extra boost, the icing on the competitive cake. In 1987, Regner came into prominence with the East German sports machine. He discovered two teenage girls, both soon to be swim sensations. Grit Mueller and Diana Block were both thirteen when Regner began his magic training regimens. Regner knew he had talent in the pool, but, as he recounted to *Der Spiegel,* he soon learned that he also had training machines, engineered by the great sports doctors of the East, including Dr. Jochen Neubauer.

Dr. Neubauer, a rising medical star, supervised training of the elite athletes at the ASK-Potsdam swim club. He orchestrated the conditioning of these young swimmers. "He called me into his office one day and told me to close the door," Regner said in his interview. "He then placed a sealed envelope on the table and told me to pay close attention. 'There are special pills here and I want you to give these to our high achievers,' he told me with a stern voice. 'They will have one-half a tab each day; you will see that it is good.' He grinned."

Inside the envelope were twelve round blue tablets, 4 mm in length. Neubauer explained to his protégé Regner that all of this was top-secret and nobody was to know, especially the athletes and their families. "We discussed the best method," Regner said in his confession. "We decided to dissolve the pills in water and mix it with their vitamins—they would never know." When Regner asked Neubauer what the pills were for, he was told, "Don't worry, I will tell you later."

Regner gave the pills to Grit Mueller and Diana Block, who were barely teenagers. He mixed the blue tabs with their vitamins, their daily intake of glucose, lemon, iron, potassium, and magnesium. The mixture was placed in plastic training bottles and brought poolside. During the next twelve days, both girls consumed 5mg of Oral-Turinabol per day, mixed gracefully into their vitamin drinks. And no one but Neubauer—and eventually Regner—knew.

One cool afternoon during a long workout, Dr. Neubauer took Regner aside and casually mentioned a few items, as if Regner were about to go to the local supermarket for groceries. "Just be mindful that our teenage girls could become a bit happy," he said to Regner with a smile. He was referring to their increased sexual urges and the premature onset of adolescent libido, a known side effect of these drugs. "If they need some help there, we can take care of that; if they are moody or become tense, then just cut back the dose," he advised Regner.

Mueller won the European championships in the 800-meter freestyle competition that year. Two days before her race, she won bronze in the 400-meter freestyle and 400-meter individual medley, with only forty minutes' rest between races. The feat was not quite human. "Only the Oral-Turinabol could account for this phenomenal training and competition schedule," Regner acknowledged. Not long after the competition, Regner had been compelled to sign a secret document, taking an oath of secrecy for knowledge of the "UM" or "supporting means," which became medical code for doping. Failure to take the oath meant severe punishment. "After I signed," Regner said, "I was part of the inner circle. I became the trainer for not only Mueller and Block, two proven stars, but also for Katrin Gronau, Heide Grein, Karin Meyer, Francisca Zietermann, and Andrea Koch. I was to get them ready physically, emotionally, and pharmacologically for the 1988 Seoul Olympics."

Two years after the Olympics, as the events leading to unification unfolded, some details for the GDR's doping program began to trickle out to the press. At that time, Michael Regner was preparing to leave Europe. Before he left, he called *Der Spiegel,* offering to give his account of the doping scheme. Soon after the interview he departed for New Zealand, where he had a promise of employment, thus avoiding any indictment or participation in the Berlin doping trials.

11

The Media and the Mentors

Der Tagesspiegel is the liberal paper of the Berlin press. Its reporters have been covering the doping trials since the beginning in March of 1998. Frank Bachner, a senior correspondent for the paper, is charming, easygoing, and not your typical German newsperson. He wears jeans and a sport jacket, without a tie, and has that disheveled look of a reporter who is overworked, underpaid, and perhaps not that well appreciated. He has provided me with background to the criminal doping case, filling in the blanks on the personalities, the names and faces of the doctors and coaches implicated in this thirty-year scandal. He knows the territory, the athletes, and their personas, and has studied their fears. "I don't know if I can get you too many interviews with the athletes at this point," he laments. "They are feeling stressed and very victimized, by everyone, including the media."

Bachner has been sending me stories and insights about the criminal trials for several years. He arranged press credentials for me at the courthouse, and seems genuinely concerned about the human side of this scandal, about the victims of the East German doping machine. We talk over lunch and then follow up our conversation at the headquarters of *Der Tagesspiegel* in downtown Berlin. His colleagues are polite, yet not particularly friendly. They seem curious, more than anything else, about this American in their midst. Bachner opens a huge drawer full of files, saying, "Here are the articles, and there is the copy machine," pointing to an old beater that had clearly seen its share of journalistic action. We talk some more and agree to stay in touch for the duration of the court proceedings.

Later that day, Professor Franke and I are due to meet at the Dubrovnik, an apt name for a quaint soup-and-salad joint across the street from the courthouse. He is late. Television crews are following him everywhere. He obliges, and our two-minute interview turns into a twenty-minute dialogue. He is making an effort to be polite, although this is a job for him.

A bit later, we hop a cab from the courthouse to the law offices of Christian Paschen and Dr. Michael Lehner. Lehner is the lead attorney for the athletes and for the Franke family. He acts a bit reserved and cautious, but knows that I'm a friend of Franke's; so he does seem eager to help. Lehner lives in Heidelberg but has law offices in several cities, including Berlin. A well-known criminal attorney, Lehner takes on high-profile cases in which clients pay large fees. His reputation for tough, thorough legal work is legendary. But for the female coplaintiffs who have retained him as counsel, he has chosen to work pro bono. He is deeply distressed about the GDR doping regime and wants his clients to have their day in court.

Lehner apologizes for his halting English as he discusses

criminal liability. "We have many obstacles to overcome, especially the statute of limitations," he says with a sense of urgency. "That will run out in October of 2000, so we must get ourselves organized quickly before our time is up." The deadline to which Lehner referred was an exceptional one in the German legal system, created as an outcome of reunification.

Under the German statutes of limitations normally applicable to the crimes with which the GDR doctors and trainers were charged, the prosecutions would have had to be commenced within five years and completed within ten years after the offenses were committed. Since these offenses were committed in the 1980s—more than ten years ago— these limitation periods would already have expired. However, concerned that persons who committed certain crimes in the GDR might evade conviction due to the lapse of the normal limitation periods, the German Parliament passed special legislation in 1993 providing that the limitation periods for the prosecution of those crimes would not expire before October 2, 2000. This legislation covers the crimes involved in the GDR doping trials.

Paschen, Lehner's younger partner, is a bit more relaxed. His English is fluent, and he doesn't apologize when he explains his agenda. "I am frustrated by the proceedings," he confesses. "I feel that in one of our cases, the Dynamo Swim Club of Berlin, the judge is not very attentive and is more focused on getting his vacation schedule in order. I also know that this particular judge is embarrassed by all of these medical atrocities and wants to get the trial behind him. Elections are coming up in Germany, and he needs to get the slate cleaned up."

Paschen readily explains his other concerns. "Some of the

judges are not taking the charges seriously enough and are only talking about fines and a slap on the wrist," he says with impatience. "I want to see some real justice, some stiff penalties and jail time and no license to practice medicine." One doctor has recently plea-bargained; he is being fined about $1,800 and is not giving up his medical license. Lehner, on the other hand, feels that perhaps the evidence will lead to some bigger fish as well as a bigger pan to fry them in. "Our clients, mainly swimmers at this point, don't want the doctors or coaches to be severely punished," he explains. "They want the medical people to just tell the truth, to give full disclosure, and to explain completely what drugs were given, and in what dosages, and what their intent was. They just want the full story. Perhaps at a later point, we can get criminal indictments against some top-level administrators and even some cabinet ministers," he suggests with a smile.

Paschen notes that to add insult to injury many of the athletes have had to submit to gynecological exams by expert witnesses to determine the damage to their bodies, including their reproductive organs. These experts have then stood up and shared this information in the public court-room. "It has been a terrible embarrassment, an extreme humiliation for these proud women," he acknowledges. "It's as if they haven't been damaged enough as teenagers, their cancerous tumors are not large enough, now we need to create more emotional metastases. And so the ladies are again victimized in the courtroom."

The lawyers have been hired by Professor Franke, who is filing separate lawsuits claiming criminal intent and fraud by his medical colleagues. Lehner and Paschen are also representing some of the athletes, including Brigitte Berendonk.

Through Berendonk, former GDR Olympians have been brought together. In standing up to the former East German coaches, trainers, and doctors, she has taken on the sports establishment as well as many leading officials of the oppressive former GDR regime. Her relentless insistence that attention be brought to this issue has made her a heroine to many of her former colleagues. Athletes from the past three decades flocked to Berendonk as she continued to speak out, and especially after she published her textbook report of the STASI files, outlining in gruesome detail the early doping experiments. Now the victims of those experiments are having their say.

12

Lothar and the Hand People

During the closing arguments of the trial of Dr. Lothar Kipke, a senior physician for all of GDR doping and the doctor responsible for Karen König's swimming career, an outburst was heard coming from a far corner of the wood-paneled courtroom. "You knew all along, you were totally aware of the effects, how it would hurt my body," came the cries from the gallery. The judge, Peter Faust, pounded his huge oak desk with the gavel and demanded order and quiet. "If I hear another outburst from you, young lady, you will be fined and removed from the proceedings," he admonished from the lofty perch of his legal bench. But it was not König, the 100-meter freestyle world record holder, who was clamoring for justice, but another competitor, Martina Gottschalt, the former 100- and 200-meter swimming champion.

She had come to the trial at the insistence of chief counsel Michael Lehner, who had filed criminal complaints on behalf of his clients, König, Gottschalt, Kornelia Ender, Petra Schneider, and other GDR champions. Today, they were there to face their tormentor, seventy-two-year-old

Lothar Kipke, M.D., the medical mastermind behind the doping of hundreds of female swimmers who brought home to East Germany some twenty Olympic titles and thirty world records between 1973 and 1989. This was the heyday of the GDR doping machine. Kipke, its chief physician, had confessed to his wrongdoings but sugar-coated his disclosure: "I had no idea at the time that there would be medical problems with these athletes," he said dismissively. Judge Faust did not agree and slammed Kipke with the heaviest penalty to date, a fine of 10,000 deutsche marks (approximately $5,743 U.S. dollars) and a fifteen-month jail sentence. Charged with fifty-four counts of administering steroids, Kipke told the court, "I was only following orders when I gave the drugs to these competitors."

Kipke had started his illustrious career in Leipzig. He became a senior sports-medicine guru, but also had major credentials outside Germany. He served on the board of FINA, the prestigious governing body for swimming under the sacred umbrella of the International Olympic Committee. His code name was "Rolf," and he wore several hats in that guise. In the larger world of sport he was known as a crusader against doping, insisting that "we must clean up the swimming drug scene." Behind the scenes, however, he wrote the protocols for the GDR master plan of performance-enhancement superiority. In 1978, he appeared in a well-known documentary film shown all over Germany, proclaiming the need to clean up sport.

But Kipke, now faced with serious jail time like the other miracle workers of the GDR, only signed a partial confession. He did not disclose the full story: that he insisted that all of his ladies be given birth-control pills to prevent pregnancy and the ugly side effects that might follow. And so when Kipke gave his confession, "I just did what they told me to do," Martina Gottschalt cried out, "Look my fifteen-year-old son in the eyes and tell him you were just following orders." Her son sat quietly next to her, his body twisted in an odd pretzel shape, squeezed into position by his deformed clubfoot, a by-product of his mother's heavy ingestion of Oral-Turinabol, the supporting means and wonder drug of the GDR. Young Gottschalt looked confused by all the commotion, his mother deeply distressed by the lies and the denials of Dr. Kipke, her mentor, her trusted father figure, and one who had many years before taken the Hippocratic Oath to heal and to do no harm.

It first occurred to another swimmer, Jutta Gottschalk, that there might be a relationship between her days as an elite athlete for the GDR and the whispers about those "vitamins" she had to swallow when her baby girl Karina was born. "I realized now for the first time that the rumors about all the crap we had to swallow in between laps was true," she said recently from her home in Dortmund, Germany. Jutta had just testified at the trial of Dr. Lothar Kipke in January of 2000, and she was hurt, angry, and confused about the years of unfinished business that seemed to come crashing all around her. "Yes, it occurred to me that Karina's blindness was related to all the steroids we took," she wept. "I was given the pills, the Oral-Turinabol, the injections, all that stuff to make us faster and tougher . . . and now I pay the ultimate price."

Gottschalk, the GDR national champion in 1978 for the 100- and 200-meter breaststroke, had a five-year tenure as one of the top swimmers from her sports club in Marteburg. She swam from 1975 through 1980, quitting her sport right before the Moscow Olympics. Now a CPA, Jutta explained that she just burned out. "I hated the way the trainers and coaches treated us in the pool. They were mean to us: the workouts were grueling," she recalled. "And on top of this, we now have to live with the legacy of the pills, another generation afflicted." Gottschalk spoke haltingly of how painful her menstrual cycles were as a result of the testosterone injections. "I could climb the walls, my period was so awful," she cried. "I had no idea it was the pills, so I told my gynecologist and he gave me birth-control pills to ease the pain."

As the GDR doping trials continued, many former champions came forward to bear witness against Lothar Kipke. "He never directly injected us; it was always somebody under his control, a low-level trainer or doctor," Jutta explained. "That is why at the trial he was able to say that he only did what he was told to do; pass on the drugs to the club trainers. Yet he knew, he knew how dangerous these drugs were." Many athletes like Gottschalk are now joining a class of civil plaintiffs and working with lawyer Michael Lehner to file separate complaints so that they can get medical attention for their children. Jutta believes there is a whole group of deformed and disabled children lining up to testify against their doctor. "I asked him in the courtroom if he would give these steroids to his children. He said prior to 1977, he would, but after that date, no, he then knew the dangers. And yet, he showed no remorse in the proceedings, he just sat there like an old, feeble man."

Gottschalk explained that it was her trainer and her doctor who gave the shots and the pills. "Kipke just walked around managing the whole scheme, and yet he claimed he was doing this to help us athletes, to make us all better people, a greater nation. Some excuse. It appeared to us in the courtroom as if a deal had been struck and that we were just going through the motions," Jutta said. "The fifteen-month suspended prison sentence and 7800 DM fine seemed like a walk in the park; it didn't seem like it was fair, not real justice. We need other families to come forward, not to feel shame or guilt but to come forward and testify in our civil suit so that we can help heal our deformed children."

Martina Gottschalt, now thirty-four and the mother of four children, all boys, seemed haunted as she described her four pregnancies. The former two-time GDR 100/200 meter backstroke champion (from 1976–1981) sounded deeply saddened and angry as she relived her past. "All four boys were difficult to conceive," she said. "All were painful and stressful pregnancies, requiring lots of hospitalizations, but my oldest was the most difficult. Daniel was born with a severely deformed foot, a clubfoot, and we have had three major surgeries already with no success. It has been financially and emotionally very tough on our family."

Gottschalt, a medical assistant in Halberstadt, Germany, was furious when speaking of Lothar Kipke. "I was so angry when I swam; we were mentally and physically abused at our swim club; and then to have to suffer a lifetime of emotional pain with the steroids and their side effects. It is overwhelming," she said. "When the police saw my name in the files, they called me and asked me to testify for the state. They knew I was just one of many victims who needed to come forward.

"I knew that my body was changing; my shoulders, the strength in my arms; but we were forbidden to speak about any of this," she said. Today, Martina suffers from a host of ailments, including debilitating back pain. She has undergone several gallbladder surgeries. And, of course, there is the struggle of fifteen-year-old Daniel. "He is severely disabled, and with all the best surgeons in Germany we have not been able to help him. We have consulted experts and there appears to be a link between the excessive testosterone levels and Daniel's deformity. In fact we know of a dozen other children with the same disability born to GDR athletes." Attorney Michael Lehner confirmed that this was indeed the case. "I think we have the scientific data to prove this relationship of the steroids to these horrible deformities," he said.

"Testifying was therapeutic for me," Martina said. "I have repressed these memories of the pain and trauma for so long. I'm glad I have the opportunity to stand in the courtroom and face my fear. And yet, Dr. Kipke did not show any remorse, he took no responsibility for his actions; he just sat there and said he had no idea about any of the side effects. Only his lawyer turned to me and personally apologized in front of the courtroom," she said with exasperation.

"I did have a moment of sweet revenge, more therapeutic perhaps. I asked Kipke to look at my son sitting there all twisted from his deformity; I asked him why he would do this to my son; he seemed embarrassed and flustered by my confrontation. I told him to apologize to my son for all the years of pain, now and into the future," she said.

There are so many dark, ugly secrets of the former GDR, Gottschalt maintained. "I think the judge is reluctant to dig too far into the past. So we settle with a fine and a suspended jail sentence. It's all very shady. Many athletes," she said quietly, "have died from the injections. We have many skeletons in our past.

"But for me, it is now out of the closet and a chance to talk about some things. I feel like I need to get some professional help to work through the emotions," Martina said. "I need some help to go beyond this and the guilt I feel about my son."

13

Voices from the Past

Kipke's trial was winding down. It was the start of the new millennium, January of 2000, and, with the statute of limitations about to run out in October, just nine months away, the GDR doping trials were coming up against a deadline. Lehner and his team of legal experts needed to move fast to process the new claims, to visit with the athlete-coplaintiffs who had just walked in to tell their stories, and to get the federal prosecutors filled in on any new cases. They needed to understand the depth of the crime: "willful intent to do bodily harm."

The trials had been under way for almost two years. So far, Michael Lehner had twelve clients with deformed children. But he knew that there were dozens of athletes who had given birth to babies with deformities, blindness, and serious organ dysfunction. Rumors were swirling that many more parents would finally relinquish their silence and come forward to bear witness. Kipke might be back in court later, even years from now, facing civil penalties, now that champion Petra Schneider had come forward with her health problems (including liver dysfunction, tumors, and internal bleeding), and now that Barbara Krause, the 100/200-meter freestyle swimming champion of the Moscow Olympics, had disclosed that she had two young daughters born with clubfeet.

And between Lehner and the judge, there was obvious tension. Lehner had a skeptical look on his face. "Did you give these young women pills, the little blue and pink ones, the Oral-Turinabol?" asked Lehner. "Yes, I did," came the reply from Kipke. "Did you give them injections of testosterone esters?" continued Lehner. "No, no injections, just pills," Kipke said.

Of course, this was not new territory that was being pursued. During the Nuremberg trials, there had been the disclosure of the use of phenol injections, referred to as "spritzen," meaning injected or squirted. The passive form of the verb, "abgespritzt," means to be injected off, or murdered through injection. So, dating from the war crimes trials, negative associations with the word for injection were quite strong in Germany. And there was also the clinical distinction: pills, it could be argued, are offered by a doctor, to be taken voluntarily by the patient, whereas an injection—whereby a needle pierces the skin, entering into muscle and blood—must be administered by a medically qualified person who has direct responsibility for delivery of the medication.

"Did you give them injections of testosterone esters?" Lehner asked again. As Kipke repeatedly denied his association with "spritzen," thus claiming only minimal responsibility for the harm done to athletes, Lehner seemed on the verge of losing his composure. He knew the limits of liability set forth by the unified Germany—as determined by the statute of limitations, the amnesty granted to many individuals, and the fact that they could not be tried for crimes committed under a regime which no longer existed—and he knew what to expect regarding the judge's ruling and the penalties that could be imposed. But he knew, too, that there was a second generation of victims coming forward.

"Dr. Kipke, you are the Joseph Mengele of the GDR doping system," he shouted at the stunned doctor. Silence and shock suddenly pervaded the courtroom. "You are the perversion of the art of curing people. How could you harm these young women, and know the consequences of these drugs?" In his final arguments to the court, Lehner addressed the frail-looking defendant directly, saying, "You are a non-doctor, and you have perverted the ethics of your profession; how is it that a doctor was given charge of young girls and offered them up as guinea pigs?"

Lehner's remarks were roundly attacked in the German press. To invoke the horrific medical experiments perpetrated by the Nazi doctors seemed out of bounds to many observers of the GDR doping trials. Certainly, the deeds of the Nazi doctors were monstrous, and to a degree far beyond those of the GDR doping doctors. But the two sets of circumstances do not seem entirely unrelated. After all, the Hippocratic oath, the pledge that all medical school graduates are required to uphold, contains the mandate, "First, do no harm." Surely, there had to be a reason why a lawyer of Lehner's stature and discretion had been provoked into making this startling analogy.

While it may be impossible to comprehend the behavior of doctors who violate so profoundly the ethics of their profession, it can be enlightening to examine some of the literature related to the practice of medicine in the Third Reich.

These trials, after all, were taking place in the context of postwar Germany. Some insight into that context can be found in the work of Robert Jay Lifton, a psychiatrist and historian whose book *The Nazi Doctors* was published in 1986. In that book, Lifton notes that "the Nazi medical idea . . . related itself to the Hippocratic Oath. The claim was that medicine had been despiritualized mainly by what Gerhard Wagner identified as the mechanically oriented spiritual Jewish teachers. There was thus a need to return to the ethics and high moral status of an earlier generation . . . which stood on solid philosophical ground of the Hippocratic Oath.

"Heinrich Himmler, the SS chief himself, embraced Hippocrates as a model for the SS physicians. In a brief introduction to a series of short books for SS doctors under the title 'Eternal Doctors,' Himmler wrote of the real Greek doctor Hippocrates," of the "unity of character and accomplishment in his life, which proclaims a morality, the strengths of which are still undiminished today and shall continue to determine medical action and thought in the future." The books were "authorized" by none other than Hitler himself.

To Lehner, the systematic doping plan could be seen as history repeating itself, a reinvention of Aryan supremacy. State Planning Theme 14.25, it could be argued, was merely a new forum for building strength, courage, and superiority through medical experiments and newly engineered athletic bodies. Likewise, Kipke's disavowal of direct responsibility for harm evoked responses given at other court proceedings nearly half a century ago.

But shortly after Kipke's trial, in late January of 2000, when I spoke with Lehner, he confessed that he had mixed feelings about his comments. "I had no intention of relating these trials to the Holocaust," he said apologetically. "My intent was to get the point across, and on the record, that these were medical experiments performed on children by a licensed practitioner of medicine." (The charge was eventually changed to "willful intent to do bodily harm to minors," thus overcoming the edict against prosecuting an individual who had committed a crime as an agent of a collapsed state.) He knew the risks, the potential fallout from his comments. "Yes, the media as well as my legal colleagues were a bit shocked by the Dr. Mengele analogy," he admitted, "but we did get their attention. During the upcoming Ewald and Höppner trials, in May 2000, I plan to tone down my rhetoric," he said wryly.

14

The GDR Learning Curve

Dr. Kipke's attempt to portray himself in court as one who had operated from a distance was hardly unusual in the context of the GDR doping program. The success of the whole system was dependent upon various mechanisms to obscure any associations between the individuals and the drugs.

From my many interviews with former GDR athletes, it was evident that disinformation had always been the key word relative to the dispensing of anabolic steroids to swimmers in the GDR. Athletes under eighteen years of age were told the "big lie"—that is, that they were being given "vitamins." Everything occurred without their knowledge. Athletes over eighteen years of age were told they were receiving "performance-enhancement supplements" and were verbally pledged to silence by their trainers. Female swimmers who were being injected with anabolic steroids were told again and again that they were receiving vitamin injections.

To prevent the athletes from stumbling across the truth on their own, they were never allowed to come into contact with the products, ampules, and packaging from VEB Jenapharm. A directive was given to distribute the drugs either rewrapped in foreign packaging, or with no packaging whatsoever, and never to allow the athletes under any circumstances to see the real pharmaceuticals. When parents of the young athletes expressed concern over the apparent changes in their children, they were simply told stories to assuage their fears.

Along with all this doping success, a major problem emerged. There were now the new testing protocols announced by the International Olympic Committee in 1974, along with the newly certified labs that checked testosterone levels and hormone thresholds. The architects of the doping program realized they could not rely on their usual methods if they were to be ready for the upcoming Olympics to be held in Montreal. Those games, slated for 1976, could be pivotal in determining whether the GDR doping program could continue without detection.

One of the documents found by Franke revealed the development of a highly refined system for organizing and recording drug testing overseen by Kipke—that eventually enabled the GDR to conquer the International Olympic Committee's own system. Following the IOC's 1974 announcement, the Central Committee of the Socialist Unity Party (Zentralkomitee ZK) had passed a nine-page top-secret initiative—State Planning Theme 14.25—that outlined steps to secure the doping protocols and testing procedures.

The 1976 games brought a huge success to the GDR, with the winning of tons of gold medals and a new sense of prestige for their homeland. This renewed validation of their athletic dominance was a tremendous boost to their political needs as well.

The push for secrecy on doping became obsessive when in 1977, Ilona Slupianek, from SC Dynamo, tested positive and was disqualified. Further cases of positive drug tests were something that the GDR sports leadership could not afford.

Due to the increased vigilance of the Olympic drug-testing protocols, GDR doctors were anxious to get their labs up to current standards. There was much anticipation about acquiring a mass spectrometer, a state-of-the-art testing device from the U.S. firm Hewlett Packard, at a cost of $187,000. With the technology of gas chromatography paired with mass spectrometry, GC/MS, the GDR would be ahead of the doping curve.

The practical knowledge of how to screen urines for uncovering illegal drug use was conveyed to the GDR by Dr. Manfred Donike, the developer of the T/E ratio test mentioned in Chapter 5. A member of the IOC medical commission, Donike was a preeminent authority in the fields of pharmacology and toxicology. Donike himself described to Manfred Höppner his process for obtaining anabolic evidence by means of mass spectrometry.

Mass spectrometry was far superior to the traditional radioimmunoassay, or RIA test, that was then in use for identifying trace evidence of the use of anabolic steroids. When the doping control laboratory acquired its own mass spectrometer in the spring of 1978, they were then in the position of being 100 percent reliable in screening their own athletes for any traces of doping.

Complete medical records of nearly all competitors were found by Franke (some are included in the appendix of this book) which documented the doping codes. Within these records lay the answer to the riddle of how detection by Olympic doping labs had been beaten.

The doping control research team in Kreischa included "external travel testing" as a requirement for all competitors. That is, no athlete of any sport was allowed to travel outside of the GDR without providing a urine sample that came back negative. The SMD in Berlin-East served as a coordinating organization on doping control and testing issues so that the timely collection of urine specimens from the athletes could be assured, whether the collection occurred at the Sport Club or at a training camp in the GDR. Dr. Höppner was responsible for coordinating all of the drug testing.

The urine specimens came in from all areas of sport, and from all areas of the GDR, by truck to Kreischa, for the purpose of these external travel tests. The samples were delivered in uniform glass bottles provided by the doping laboratory. Each specimen was identified by a code number, with an abbreviation indicator (for example, LA for Light Athletics) to show the sport affiliation of the specimen donor, but not the name. All of the specimens delivered were accompanied by a list, from which the code numbers, by means of the sport event abbreviations and the place of origin of the specimen, could be read.

With typical German precision, every specimen delivered was recorded in a urine-test logbook, along with the code number and another code number assigned and modified by the laboratory. The doping laboratory in Kreischa was required to comply with strict security regulations.

The specimens were delivered directly into a specially secured area; they were then no longer accessible to any one individual. Positive tests, that is, tests which were found to contain doping substances, were also entered into a separate record, which was archived. Only the director of the doping laboratory, Dr. Clausnitzer, had full access to these protocols.

The results of doping tests from Kreischa were transmitted directly to Dr. Höppner at SMD, typically with a telephone call to provide advance notification, followed by a written report. Only Dr. Clausnitzer and his deputy were authorized to transport the findings to Berlin.

This filing procedure was accomplished on the basis of the record that was created when the urine specimen was collected. The athlete preparing to provide the specimen was presented with a prewritten protocol record bearing his or her name and a seven-place code number of which he or she was given a carbon copy. One copy of the protocol record was sent from the collection site directly to Berlin to the SMD, while the specimen itself with another carbon copy of the protocol, containing only the code number, and not the name of the athlete, was sent to Kreischa for processing.

If a doping test returned positive, one of two procedures would be applied: if there were still a few days remaining before the scheduled departure of the athlete, then multiple urine specimens would be collected at intervals, until they returned a negative result. If a negative result was not returned before the departure, then that athlete was denied travel permission, effectively removing him or her from that competition. Many times a doctor would take the athlete on the trip anyway, on his own responsibility, in the hope that the doping value readings would be negative prior to the actual competition.

One big problem for the doping laboratory in Kreischa was that the tests were arranged to occur as close to the travel date as possible. This situation arose because the medical personnel at the sport clubs had an interest in continuing dosages of doping medication for as long as possible right up until the athletes' departure. This often created a bottleneck situation, where a large quantity of urine specimens arrived for testing just hours before the planned departure.

Along with external travel testing prior to competitions abroad, there was also a national testing program at certain times of the year. Along with these work responsibilities, the Kreischa laboratory also performed contract testing for doping substances for other countries and athletes outside of Germany—giving rise to a new cottage industry for the GDR.

One serious setback for "supportive means" and the drug-imbued GDR women's swimming organization occurred during preparations for the Swimming World Championships in 1978 in Berlin-West. This was a pivotal event, where the use of Turinabol-Depot ampules from Jenapharm led to a grave breakdown. The doping control laboratory in Kreischa already had the mass spectrometer in 1978, and was therefore in a position to identify and isolate the most minute traces of anabolic steroids and metabolites in a urine specimen to a level of 100 percent reliability. However, during a routine testing period just prior to the swimming championships, a total of thirteen swimmers were tested, and ten tested positive for illegal substances. After the first repeat test on a new urine specimen, two swimmers, Petra Thümer and Christiane Sommer, tested positive again. The tests revealed that they were both on the drug Nandrolone, which could only have come from an injection of a Nandrolone Depot preparation. This meant that eight weeks before the start of the World Championships, these female swimmers had been injected with intramuscular doses of this powerful performance-enhancement drug.

The two swimmers had to travel to Kreischa, where they submitted urine specimens every twelve hours, but, over and over, the tests came back positive. Consequently, Petra Thümer and Christiane Sommer did not travel to the World Championships in Berlin, but remained in the GDR. The rumor was circulated that they were suffering from the flu and were too sick to compete.

This fiasco, brought about because of the poor timing of drug use, showed the GDR sport leadership how vulnerable they were.

New research was now under way to better time the injections. Up until the summer of 1978, it was believed that injections of Depot-Turinabol were cleared from the body in thirty days, and that the ingestion of Oral-Turinabol tablets was no longer found after fourteen days. It was on the basis of these assumptions that the timing and sequencing of administration of Depot-Turinabol and Oral-Turinabol had been established. After consultations, the research group on supportive means from FKS, in cooperation with the association doctors, released a new guideline stating that the Depot-Turinabol injections should cease thirty days before the competition and that Oral-Turinabol should cease fourteen days before the competition.

Awareness of this fact influenced the method for dispensing anabolic steroids to young athletes. The GDR plan had been initially to administer Depot-Turinabol preparations, and then, in the later phases before competition, to switch to tablets, such as the Oral-Turinabol. On the basis of what was learned in 1978 concerning the time required to fully eliminate anabolic preparations from the body, changes in doping for sport had to be made.

The drug doctors issued a directive to halt use of these doping preparations. Shifting gears, they temporarily suspended all GDR doping. As a result, the GDR national women's swimming team performed poorly at the 1978 Swimming World Championships in Berlin, and lost the position of leadership that they had gained at the 1976 Montreal Olympics.

The reason that the "doping fiasco" involving swimmers Thümer and Sommer could occur, in spite of the lessons learned in April or May 1978 concerning the lengthy time required to eliminate the Depot-Turinabol, was that Dr. Kipke had not immediately informed all of the section doctors about the extensive drug testing. It was the first major black mark on his stellar career. After the 1978 Swimming World Championships the GDR plan changed and new timetables were implemented.

It was the first, but not the last, period of adjustment for the GDR doping machine.

The major mystery of how the GDR doping program managed to beat the drug tests unfolded as more documents spilled out of the STASI archives. After drug testing had started to bounce GDR competitors out of the ring, a new system had emerged. In order to taper individual synthetic steroids from the body, trainers would cut back several weeks prior to competition. To enable young athletes to maintain intense training workouts, the doctors would inject them with testosterone esters, a substitute for the steroids, but a compound that was undetectable by standard testing procedures. The "esters" would be part of a "bridge-therapy" to get the competitors through the testing period without getting busted. The "esters" would keep their hormone levels high, but blend with their natural body hormones and not reveal the previous doping pills. In fact, Dr. Clausnitzer conducted a study of 241 athletes to determine the effectiveness of these "bridge-esters" and found that within three days of the injections the T/E ratio (the standard formula for detecting drug-induced performances) would be back to normal levels.

But GDR doping experts were not satisfied with just one safeguard, so the scientists came up with another measure to protect the secrecy of their doped competitors. They went back to their colleagues at Jenapharm and came up with a new compound, epitestosterone, a biologically inactive compound (found naturally in all human beings) that would be injected at the right training cycle to bring the 6:1 ratio down to acceptable levels for drug control. Another German miracle of science.

When all else failed, STASI documents revealed, urines would be switched, stolen from the bona fide athlete, to be substituted by a pure urine from a noncompetitor, a practice that is well-known and widespread in the United States. The pure urine would either be infused by a catheter into the competitor's bladder (a rather painful procedure) or be held in condoms until it was time to give a specimen to the drug control lab.

These STASI files, including all drug tests, were kept in

Berlin and in Kreischa at the research hospital and at the ZDKL lab (an IOC accredited lab) under the direction of Dr. Clausnitzer. This lab was not only an IOC lab but also the "clearinghouse" for all GDR urines, a small blemish on the IOC medical commission, whose members deny that they even knew anything about German doping procedures.

However, there were more deeply disturbing revelations, as Professor Franke discovered. In addition to the miracle drug, Oral-Turinabol, some athletes received a combination of substances, including a dose of mestanolone. A steroid derivative, mestanolone was only available as an experimental preparation in the early 1980s from the ZIMET lab. The experimental protocol was given to female gymnasts and handball and volleyball players, without approval for human use, not even clinical phase I trials. In one of the more disturbing reports of systematic doping, Franke learned that the renowned drug guru Manfred Höppner had a conscience. Evidently, Höppner got nervous about this unproven preparation and reported to his superiors at the STASI that "he would not be responsible for the medical consequences of this untested drug."

But Franke became more distressed as he uncovered the most sordid details of the scheme. According to one classified document, Dr. Höppner had informed the STASI that women who had been on the program and later became pregnant could experience malformations of the fetus. This warning was written in 1977. Höppner, due to stand trial in May 2000, would no doubt be grilled on these early disclosures. Furthermore, in 1984 Höppner had referred ten athletes for hospitalization and discovered that they had severe liver damage. One athlete, Detlef Gerstenberg, a

1980 Olympic hammer thrower, was hospitalized at age thirty-five with extensive liver damage and an obstruction in his bile duct. He died in 1993 from postoperative complications. At his funeral, one of his fellow teammates admitted that he, too, had serious liver problems.

Other problems have emerged as well. One side effect from prolonged use of Oral-Turinabol is gynecomastia, or breast enlargement in males. At the cancer hospital in Berlin, twelve weight lifters recently underwent a surgical procedure to reduce their breasts and enlarged nipples. One of those weight lifters, Roland Schmidt, has taken his case to the German courts and is part of the civil action that is presently under way.

In locating State Planning Theme 14.25, Franke unveiled the most profound archival evidence that decisions on doping in sport were made at the highest government level. This paper was the working document for UM, "supporting means," the euphemism for the doping of all competitors. The plan was to be coordinated out of Leipzig and financed by special government grants. Disturbing as its contents were, this document gave firepower to the prosecutors, opening the door to massive indictments.

15

Central Casting

One of those Olympians who confided in fellow competitor Brigitte Berendonk was Rica Reinisch. With Brigitte's moral support, she was preparing for her first court appearances in 1998.

After winning gold in Moscow in 1980, Reinisch felt a new sense of accomplishment and pride in her homeland. After all, she was a hero in the GDR. Gold medals brought one fame and fortune. They also brought tremendous glory to a nation with a very low self-image. Perhaps that is why one could deny pain and suffering, and accept the swallowing of little pills to make it all go away.

Reinisch knew that her swim times were getting faster by the week, her training more intense, and her recovery from daily workouts a lot easier. On a conscious level, her speed, her drive, her performance were all that mattered. But she knew on some subliminal level that her young, sexy teenage body did not belong to her, but was being reengineered by the East German sports machine. She knew that chemicals were interacting with her natural athletic abilities to produce superhuman performances.

"I was traveling in Russia when I first noticed the intense pain," she said a few months before she was to testify, "and I went to a doctor to have it checked out. Then when I got home, I went to a specialist in Dresden, and she diagnosed the problem as ovarian cysts. It was very scary," she recalled. "I knew then what I had suspected for many years: the drugs those doctors were giving me were affecting my health."

After an illustrious swim career capped off with a gold medal and some other records, Reinisch quit the sport in 1982. She was all of sixteen years of age. "I knew there were some weird things going on within my body and with my other swimming buddies," she said in her deep voice, seeming reluctant to spill it all. "I tried to talk to other athletes about the pills, but no one wanted to talk. It was the big ugly secret. The younger athletes did not know; they seemed truly in the dark. By contrast, the older athletes seemed to be aware of the vitamins and told me not to talk about it, that it was just a training secret. Some of my older teammates said, why complain, if the pills make you train harder and swim faster . . . why do you need to complain about it, don't you want to win?"

Winning came with a price, as it always does. For Rica Reinisch that price was high. Today, she lives not only with ovarian cysts, but, more significantly, a serious heart condition, recently diagnosed. Her arrhythmia has been tied to heavy testosterone loads, loads that a female body cannot tolerate. "It was a tough situation, and I didn't know how to deal with it," she said remorsefully. "Looking back, I remember the love and respect I had for my trainer and the special bond I had with my coach. My parents were not around. We did not have family; we were isolated. Our family were the athletes and the doctors, the pool our community. They were our mentors; we had to trust them," she recalled. "I think my parents knew what was going on, but they were caught in a tough position, with my success and the prestige bestowed on our family. It was a very sick system, a catch-twenty-two, and we were all trapped deep in the heart of it."

Reinisch admitted that she felt confused by all of the doping trials. She shared her intimate feelings of being exploited and abused. And yet, Reinisch does not want to be viewed as a victim; she wants all German athletes to stand up and take responsibility for their collective behavior. "I don't want to walk into a criminal court hearing and point fingers at the doctors or trainers," she said with some resentment. "I want the doctors to stand up and disclose all, to tell the full story of what happened. Then let's have our government leaders come to court to testify about their role in this corrupt system. I still don't understand how these officials could do these horrendous things to young athletes, I don't understand how they could intentionally hurt us. 'Steigt über Leichen,' " she blasts out in German. "I don't know how the politicians could climb over corpses . . . to get gold medals!"

Rica felt that it was time for those officials to come forward and give full disclosure. "After all"—she sighed—"we were just diplomats in training suits in the old GDR."

At twenty-nine years of age, Sylvia Gerasch is considered the old lady of world-class swimming—a very quick old lady, I should add. Gerasch won gold medals in 1986 in the 100-meter breaststroke and the 4×100 medley relay. In 1998, she finished at the top in the world championships in Perth, Australia. With one eye focused on Sydney in the late summer of 2000, and the other eye on the darkest episode in the history of international amateur sports, Gerasch is unique among today's German swimmers.

When called to testify in the Berlin doping trials, Gerasch fought a subpoena and got a court order to prevent an expert gynecologist from examining her prior to her testimony. Subsequently, the procedure for determining damage to the reproductive system was changed.

Caught in the cross fire of the bad-guy East German sports machine and the new cleaned-up ethic of unified Germany's athletics, Gerasch has struggled with her identity. She has been confused and somewhat upset with her friend Brigitte Berendonk. "I think the athletes who have been harmed, severely damaged, should come forward," she said hesitantly. "I think that we need 100 percent proof of this harm, the doping and what it did to my fellow swimmers. And those who hurt us should be punished. But," she said a bit defensively, "I also think that the press is making us out to be very evil people, as if everyone in the GDR was doped and that we were the only athletes in the world who ever cheated."

When Gerasch did finally take the stand in the Dynamo Berlin trial, she virtually choked on the highly charged atmosphere of the courtroom. "I was given pills, but I threw them away," she told the prosecutor. "I did everything I could to stay in the pool and yet not swallow those little pink and blue things. . . . I knew they were trying to dope me; I knew that it was wrong," she testified.

As the only athlete involved in the GDR doping trials who is still competing, Gerasch is under enormous psychological pressure. She is constantly barraged by the media, who suspect her of doping and cite her most recent positive test for high caffeine levels. For that, she got herself a two-year suspension. There are additional suspicions of her steroid use, but she has said that she wants to be exonerated and wants to continue her swim career. She is in the delicate position of knowing all and yet only disclosing the pieces of the steroid puzzle that will keep her out of trouble. She is annoyed, too, about the rumors surrounding her past, present, and future Olympic career. "Because I still train many hours each day, it is difficult to stay focused," she said. "The media tend to exaggerate my situation and knowledge of drugs. They don't lie, they just distort the truth."

Gerasch is faced with a dilemma. On the one hand, she knows more than we will ever know about doping of athletes. Yet her conscience only allows for small doses of information to leak out. "You see, not all athletes were treated by the doctors in the same fashion. There were different standards for each athlete," she said, choosing her words carefully. "I had allergies, so I was treated differently." In June of 1998, Sylvia Gerasch was not so careful and got herself into some trouble. After she testified in the Dynamo Berlin trial that she received Oral-Turinabol and threw the pills away, Gunar Werner, chief of FINA, read her the riot act—or more precisely, the rule book. Medical rule DC9.6 states that "any athlete aware of illegal doping must report it to the IOC or other governing bodies." Though she took the pills in the old regime, as an active athlete she is bound by the federation to obey the rules of the new government. As a result, FINA has threatened her with a lifelong ban from swimming.

Brigitte Berendonk still gets phone calls from former athletes, competitors from the "other side." They want to talk, but they need someone they can trust, someone whose support will enable them to come forward to bear witness. It is not an easy choice. Words must be crafted with care, thoughts must be organized, and feelings need to be buffered. There is much emotion and trauma among the girls of the former GDR. They are now grown women with careers, with families, with responsibilities. And with grave medical problems.

16

The Showdown at High Noon

In August of 1998, East met West in a dramatic showdown in a wood-paneled courtroom in Berlin. Two sports medicine doctors of the former East Germany stood before a judge and explained how they systematically administered steroids to young girls, Olympic swim hopefuls of the GDR.

Dr. Dorit Rösler, fifty years old, told the court in disquieting detail how certain athletes received blue pills on one day, pink ones on other days. "We documented all of this: the pills, the time of day, the training regimens. It was all recorded," she said, choking back emotion. The chilling confession echoed throughout the courtroom filled with lawyers, doctors, experts from the fields of sport and medicine, and the media. The echo was heard throughout Germany and rebounded to the courtroom gallery filled with athletes who had been the subjects of this calculated medical experiment.

The spectators heard Dr. Rösler finish her story. And then, in a startling twist, her eyes brimming with tears,

Rösler turned to several athletes. "I can only repeat my profound regret," she said, her voice trembling. "I was far too
obedient. We were pressured into producing for the political leadership. We had to create international champions
for the glory of the communist sporting machine," she
cried.

Rösler's colleague, Dr. Ulrich Sünder, also testified the same
day, asserting, "We had a political function in the struggle
between the two systems. We went along with this struggle
without questioning the dangers, the fallout." Sünder
pleaded guilty to inflicting bodily harm on young teenage
athletes and was sentenced to a jail term and a small fine.
But in his heart, the sixty-year-old orthopedic surgeon
didn't really believe he deserved more than a light slap on
the wrist. "I was the chief of the Sports Medical Service, sort
of a supervisor," he said with an air of arrogance in February
of 2000 from his home outside Berlin. "I really didn't have
much to do with giving pills or sticking needles into young
arms," he asserted. "I just took orders from the top guns
and passed along the training protocols to the swim doctors
and other sports trainers."

Since 1971, Dr. Ulrich Sünder had supervised the massive buildup of GDR Olympic superiority across fourteen
different sports. His was a middle-management position,
just mid-level enough to enable him to shift the blame to
both the top officials and the doctors who actually performed the dirty work. "I can only be sentenced once, so
now I can testify against the others, but my work in court is
finished," he said dispassionately.

As Sünder saw it, some athletes had a very positive experience in the GDR, while others left sport and were bitter. "Some of our elite athletes knew they were being doped," he explained, and "since they were doing well in competition, it was no problem. On the other hand, others didn't train well, didn't compete well, and didn't tolerate the drugs very well, so they left in bitterness." He claimed that many parents were aware of the blue and pink Oral-Turinabol anabolics and the injections, "but they chose to look the other way, as long as their child was winning."

Sünder acknowledged that he did know the medical literature and that he knew about the side effects of the androgens. "But I was told by my medical superiors that the deep voice and the hair and the virilization would reverse after the women stopped taking them, so we did not worry about long-term consequences." To add insult to injury, he contended that everyone in the modern sport world, including the Americans, were doping the hell out of their athletes, "so why should we not compete on that level playing field?"

Sünder continued with his rationale. "Yes, I am a doctor with strong Olympic credentials. But you must understand that sport was a part of politics, and with this connection comes special privileges for coaches and athletes and their families," he said smugly. "We knew that Jenapharm was doing the research," he added, "so we left it to the experts to inform us if there were problems."

Sünder boasted about the training regimens, the six to eight hours of intense training in all of the sports that he supervised, but the swimmers themselves, he conceded, were unbelievable. "Their muscle mass was enormous, and their recovery from strenuous workouts was remarkable," he recalled. "Yes, those hormones did quite a job for our competitions, and most handled the drugs very well." While

Sünder described some of the problems in clinical detail, in the same breath he made it clear that this was the protocol; there was no other way to compete. "At my trial, the experts tried to prove that there was this relationship between the steroids and cancer and heart disease. It is very hard to prove; we have scientists who can stand up in court and disprove all these effects," he said with a whiff of disdain.

When prodded about "medical experiments" and "manipulating young bodies," Sünder's response was, "Yes the moral issue is clear, we were wrong. But we really didn't believe under our system that anyone would be hurt."

Throughout pointed questioning, Sünder maintained his equanimity. "In the final analysis, the media, the German people, they don't care. There is waning interest in the press. It was a long time ago; people don't care about ten or twenty years ago in the East. They know that everyone uses drugs in the Tour de France and in China and Australia and, of course, in America, so why should anyone pay attention to our doping trials," he protested. "It was in the past."

The testimony of the two doctors against the backdrop of this previously war-torn city of Berlin seemed all too familiar.

Karen König, a superstar swimmer from the 1980s, was there in Room 700 to hear Rösler and Sünder. She had been in France, moving on with her life and with a new career, when she got the call to come home.

Since her days as a GDR wunderkind in the pool, König, now thirty-one, has been very busy. She has been living in Paris, completing her master's degree in comparative literature, and planning to earn a Ph.D. with the ultimate goal of becoming a professional journalist. She has many important stories to tell.

From the age of thirteen König knew only one environment, the swimming pool, and she was told she had to swim as fast as she could. As a GDR swim champion from 1982 through 1987, she set a world record in the 4×100-meter freestyle and was the 1985 European gold medalist.

König knew she was a great athlete but didn't understand why her body was going through such dramatic changes. "I did not really know the whole story until 1990," she told me recently. "That was when we had a reunion with three other swimmers and our coach and he told us about the pills. I was totally shocked. Then I got a copy of the Berendonk book about doping, as a present from a doctor who was concerned about my health. Then, with all the media attention, I started to keep a diary of all this, and then over the past several years all the pieces fit together," she said. "It finally dawned on me that we were just guinea pigs in this big doping scheme, and then I realized that I needed to come forward and to speak up about all of the drug use."

Speaking of her years as a teenager in the swim program, König recalled that there was always fear in the pool, it was part of the training regimen. "The pills and the fear were part of our training diet," she said. "The coaches intimidated us in so many ways. I always felt like a little girl who could never grow up; I also had this sense of victimization." König would leave the pool each day in tears and shaking violently. Finally, in 1982, after asking for many months, she was allowed to see a therapist for her anxiety and depression. In counseling, she tried to sort out her confusion and trauma and her coaches' wrath. But then she suddenly quit therapy. "I found out very quickly that there was no vocabulary in the GDR for privacy or confidentiality; the shrink told all my secrets to the STASI police and to the coaches and trainers. I had no way of getting help!" she said. "Thinking back on all this, I now realize that most of this could be attributed to the imbalance in my system. The drugs were driving me crazy; I was moody and a complete basket case. I started to gain lots of weight, so I went on a diet, and I was embarrassed about this, so I withdrew from my friends. I was so isolated, it was very painful."

After she quit swimming, König tried to bury herself in her studies, to get out of Germany and to start believing in her new career. But then the dreams came. They were dreams of not having her suit on, of not being ready to compete. The dreams were filled with fear and anxiety, a sort of nakedness at the edge of the pool. "I think that once I realized what was happening, all of the images of the pills and the needles and the coaches shouting at us to perform, it all hit very hard," she told me in Berlin in February of 2000. König first testified in the Rolf Gläser trial in the summer of 1998, after she was encouraged by her peers to come forward. "I felt a sense of power in all of this," she said confidently. "I felt strong and no longer a victim, once I came forward."

König's "coming-out party" was an important step, not only to set the record straight, but also to begin her healing. She began to speak in court and to the media, and she got lots of support from her friends. "It's been a major step in my growth, to be able to defend myself and speak out against these atrocities," she said. The turning point in this process was a rather bizarre letter that she received from a

GDR swimmer Andrea Pollack, 1980 competition.
Photo: Bundesarchiv, Bild 183/W030912

GDR swimmer
Birgit Meineke,
1983 competition.
Photo:
Bundesarchiv, Bild
183/1983/0828/6

Left to right: GDR swimmers Andrea Pollack, Caren Metschuk, and Christiane Knacke, 1980 Moscow Olympics. Photo: Bundesarchiv, Bild 183/W0724/126

Left to right: GDR swimmers Monika Seltmann, Carola Nitschke, Andrea Pollack, and Barbara Krause, 1976 competition. Photo: Bundesarchiv, Bild 183/R0605/10

Left to right: GDR swimmers Cornelia Polit, Rica Reinisch, and Birgit Treiber, 1980 Moscow Olympics. Photo: Bundesarchiv, Bild 183/W0727/138

Left to right: Trainer Horst Kleefeld with GDR swimmers Barbara Krause and Andrea Pollack, 1978 competition. Photo: Bundesarchiv, Bild 183/T0821/21

Left to right: Trainer Rolf Gläser and GDR swimmer Birgit Meineke, 1981 competition. Photo: Bundesarchiv, Bild 183/Z0701/33

Left to right: Trainer Rolf Gläser with GDR swimmers Andrea Pollack and Christiane Knacke, 1978 competition. Photo: Bundesarchiv, Bild 183/T0128/27

Left to right: GDR swimmers Heike Witt, Barbara Krause, Caren Metschuk, and Petra Priemer, 1978 competition. Photo: Bundesarchiv, Bild 183/T0826/34

Left to right: GDR swimmers Andrea Pollack and Christiane Knacke, 1978 competition. Photo: Bundesarchiv, Bild 183/T0703/34

GDR swimmer
Silke Horner,
1988 Seoul
Olympics.
Photo: AP/Wide
World Photos

Left to right: American four-time Olympian Janet Evans with GDR
swimmers Heike Friedrich and Anke Moehring, 1988 Seoul Olympics.
Photo: AP/Wide World Photos

GDR swimmer
Kristin Otto, 1988
Seoul Olympics.
Photo: AP/Wide
World Photos

Left to right: GDR swimmers Birte Weigang, Kristin Otto, and Chinese swimmer Qian Hong, 1988 Seoul Olympics. Photo: AP/Wide World Photos

GDR swimmer
Kristin Otto,
1988 Seoul Olympics.
Photo: AP/Wide
World Photos

GDR swimmer
Daniela Hunger,
1988 Seoul Olympics.
Photo: AP/Wide
World Photos

Left to right: GDR swimmers Ute Geweniger, Andrea Pollack, Rica Reinisch, and Caren Metschuk, 1980 Moscow Olympics.
Photo dpa/ZB Fotoagentur Zentralbild GmbH

Federal Judge Hansgeorg Bräutigam, 1992.
Photo: dpa Deutsche Presse–Agentur GmbH

West German Olympian Brigitte Berendonk, 1972 Munich Olympics.
Photo: dpa/ZB Fotoagentur Zentralbild GmbH

GDR swimmer
Sylvia Gerasch,
1997 competition.
Photo: dpa/ZB
Fotoagentur
Zentralbild GmbH

GDR swimmer Christiane Knacke-
Sommer, 1998 court appearance.
Photo: dpa/ZB Fotoagentur
Zentralbild GmbH

GDR swimmer Karen König,
1998 court appearance.
Photo: dpa/ZB Fotoagentur
Zentralbild GmbH

Convicted GDR swim doctor Ulrich Sünder, 1998 court appearance. Photo: dpa/ZB Fotoagentur Zentralbild GmbH

GDR swimmer Andrea Pollack, 1998 court appearance. Photo: dpa/ZB Fotoagentur Zentralbild GmbH

GDR swimmer
Andrea Pollack,
1998 court appearance.
Photo: dpa/ZB
Fotoagentur Zentralbild
GmbH

Left to right: GDR swimmers Christiane Knacke-Sommer and Birgit Heike-Matz,
1998 court appearance. Photo: dpa/ZB Fotoagentur Zentralbild GmbH

Convicted GDR
doping administrator
Manfred Höppner,
2000 court appearance.
Photo: dpa Deutsche
Presse–Agentur GmbH

Convicted GDR
doping administrator
Manfred Ewald,
2000 court appearance.
Photo: dpa Deutsche
Presse–Agentur GmbH

Left to right: Prominent Berlin attorney Dr. Michael Lehner and West German Olympic champion Dieter Baumann, 2000 court appearance.
Photo: dpa Deutsche Presse–Agentur GmbH

GDR swimmer Rica Reinisch, 1980 Moscow Olympics.
Photo: dpa/ZB Fotoagentur Zentralbild GmbH

GDR swimmer
Rica Reinisch, 1997.
Photo: dpa/ZB
Fotoagentur
Zentralbild GmbH

Prominent U.S. sports lawyer and
German scholar David Ulich, 2000.
Photo: Sheppard Mullin law firm,
Los Angeles

Anti-doping advocate and author
Brigitte Berendonk, 1998.
Photo: Meyer Fotografie

recently convicted GDR doctor. With the blessings of his defense lawyer, Dr. Horst Tausch sent König a "letter of apology." "It was a joke," König laughed. "It was a combination of a mild confession, a manipulation of the facts, and a very weak apology for sticking me with needles full of anabolics. Dr. Tausch thought he could impress the judge by apologizing to his victims before the trial. It was such a sick joke."

König wanted justice to be served. She was awaiting the stiff penalties and the fines and the jail time. But mostly, she wanted the parents with disabled children to be compensated. "I believe the German government has a huge responsibility in helping with the medical costs and the rehabilitation of all these deformed children. They need to come forward and provide funding here," she said. König was not sure she will ever be able to have children, but her main fear had to do with the dreams. She wanted to heal, to finish this dark chapter in her life and be able to sleep at night. She wanted to have dreams that didn't take her back to the darkness of her teenage years, ones that would offer hope for her new career.

In a moment filled with tension, König, with the judge's permission, confronted Dr. Rösler in the courtroom. "How could you do this to us, and would you have given steroids to your children?" she cried.

"It's something I have asked myself time and time again," Rösler said haltingly, her voice quivering. "I believe that at that time in the East I would have done so!"

Both doctors admitted under oath that they prescribed and administered the pills, the Oral-Turinabol, the little pink and blue vitamins. They stopped short of acknowledging giving *injections* of hormones. The physical act of injecting a body with dangerous drugs that might cause bodily harm carries a different penalty under German criminal law.

"As a human being and as a medical doctor I have had to come to terms with this dark secret," Dr. Rösler said in a recent interview. "Before the trial, I was very depressed and I looked in the mirror and said to myself . . . how could I do this?" she said in an anguished tone. "I used the trial to come to terms with my guilt and my wrongdoing. I went into the pits, to the very bottom with all of this," she admitted. Rösler went on to say that the trials were the lowest point in her life, but a cathartic point as well. "I know that I did terrible damage to these young women, these teenagers. I lied and covered up the truth about the drugs and now I am ready to take full responsibility. I bear a double responsibility, as both doctor and their friend," she said boldly.

To this day, Rösler does not understand why so many doctors and senior sport officials are still in denial, suppressing the truth about doping and the dangers of the chemicals. "I have friends who tell me that if I had not injected these teenage swimmers . . . someone else would have stepped in and replaced me. Of course, that was the same excuse used during the Third Reich, that if we didn't respond to Hitler, another doctor would have fulfilled the function. I should have shown more courage," she said with sorrow. "In Nazi Germany we did what we were told to do. The GDR doping machine was no different; we were just carrying out our medical orders, never questioning the system that was good to us, just doing our job. Have we not learned anything?"

Rösler admitted that she first understood how dangerous the drugs were when Karen König went to the federal prosecutor in 1993 and put forth the accusation that led to Rösler's indictment for doing bodily harm. "It was then that I realized the seriousness of the crime. This was followed by a horrible article in *Der Spiegel* where König called me a pig and other unpleasant names," she explained. Although not defensive but rather full of remorse and pain about her own conduct, Rösler did relate an interesting anecdote from the dark days of GDR doping. "At one point I did have an athlete who was not well, who had very low energy and was not performing well. So I ordered some tests and I found that this swimmer had an increased liver count, and I referred this athlete to some specialists and to a hospital for treatment. I learned later that the STASI police found out and intervened. They removed the medical records from the hospital so that the parents and others would never know." Rösler recalled that some doctors did stand up and report adverse side effects and "they were removed from the GDR swim federation. They lost their contract and their prestige in the medical community, but they held their honor."

This tragic tale has a rather bizarre yet satisfying ending. Dr. Rösler, convicted doper and injector of harmful anabolic steroids, is still practicing medicine. "Yes, I still work with athletes. In fact, many athletes from the past including those who are suffering from the steroids, still come to me," she said with an awkward smile. "They trust me. I offer my services, I want to make amends, so I tell them to visit me and I treat them. We have established a new and trusting relationship. I know their parents, and I have apologized to their families, so they come to me for treatment. It is a healing for me, for both of us. I want to do something for these kids that I harmed."

Rösler is highly unusual. She is a rare doctor, person, healer, citizen of the former GDR. Most have not admitted, or only partially admitted, any wrongdoing. Many blame the system or blame their superiors. Dorit Rösler is full of shame and humiliation and wants to right the wrong. She wants to reinstate her allegiance to the Hippocratic Oath as a medical practitioner. "I am still living this nightmare," she pleads, "but I want to make amends. I also want to see the German government pay medical expenses for these deformed children. That is the very least we can do."

17

Justice Is Served

In the muggy days of a rather unusual Berlin summer, many other athletes have paraded before the witness stand in the old courthouse. They were all connected to Brigitte Berendonk, their mentor. One of these was Carola Beraktschjan. She was the 1976 world champion and Olympian in the 100-meter breaststroke and was known in her swimming days as Carola Nitschke.

As a former world record holder (a distinction that may have to be relinquished), Carola explained in her testimony the double bind that she experienced as a GDR athlete. She had instructions from her parents not to touch the pills for any reason. So she disposed of them, hid them, and threw them in the trash when her trainer, Rolf Gläser, wasn't looking. When Gläser discovered that she was not obeying the "vitamin regimen," she was asked to leave the pool. She did take some steroids, but told the court that she tried her best to avoid the pills. Her swim times rose precipitously and she was no longer part of the elite East German program.

Carola Beraktschjan has had a recurring dream for over

twenty years. "I have this image in my brain that I'm wearing my sweats right before the World Championships and I go up to the starting blocks and I can't get my clothes off and I can't start my race. I'm locked up at the blocks. When I testified in the Binus doping trial in 1998, I found out that many of my former swim buddies had the same dream. They were stuck in the blocks. They couldn't start, and if they did, they felt like they might drown."

This nightmare is now a memory. Life has moved forward for this GDR champion and mother of a thirteen-year-old girl. "I was a tough competitor, but also very stubborn," Carola recalled after the Kipke trial. "I used to love my swimming, but then the drugs came and the injections, and I said no." Carola's stubborn attitude may have saved her life. After a few months of ingesting the performance enhancements, Carola had gained twenty kilos (more than forty-five pounds) and put on huge shoulder mass. She loved her swim times, but hated the way she felt. As she improved, they moved her into the elite group of swimmers and into the heavy doping protocols. "I just woke one day and said this feels like shit. It's wrong, it's cheating, and I feel horrible. When I said no, no more pills, no more needles, the coaches freaked out. They kept trying to convince me to dope, but I refused. Shortly afterward, my performances fell behind my other training partners, so they moved me into the lazy group. I was no longer a member of GDR elite. There was fighting and arguing and it got ugly, so in 1979, right before Moscow, I just quit. Hung up my suit.

"I knew we were on something," she continued. "Everybody was getting enormous, and we are talking about young women, teenagers, here; so we all knew that we were being doped, but we were forbidden to talk to anyone or to each other. It was like prison," she said. "I got called before the

Central Committee, the big STASI honchos; they wanted me to take the vitamins and keep swimming; but I told them forget it, it was wrong and dangerous. They thought I was nuts, so they cut me loose. I also believe that some of the young girls loved the way their swim times dropped and their recovery from hard workouts, so they didn't complain; they rather enjoyed it."

Carola does not suffer from the physical ailments and disabilities that many of her colleagues do; she does not have cancer or gynecological problems. Although she suffered a traumatic loss with the tragic death of her young husband in a car crash, she is a well-adjusted woman who is ready to get on with her life. "I was not going to get involved in the doping trials. I had closed that chapter in my life. But when my doctor was indicted for doing criminal harm to my friends, I knew that wounds were about to open up." Carola was not going to join the plaintiffs until she read that her friends were being attacked. The defense attorneys and their medical experts "started accusing the swimmers of being the dopers, saying that the docs had no knowledge of the drugs." She became furious, and when her fellow champion Christiane Knacke-Sommer was being "blindsided by the legal system," she said, "I had to join the fight."

In the courtroom, the stubborn competitor in her again rose to the occasion. This time the passion was outside the pool and in the halls of justice. Carola faced her former doctor and told him that he had contaminated the pool, the swim arena, and the whole ethic of sport. "I told the court that I was giving up my medals, my world records, and sending them back, that they were tainted, spoiled, rotten symbols of a toxic society. I didn't want that in my closet. The medals don't belong to me, so I wrapped them up and sent them back to FINA, the swim federation. The medals belong to those who were clean, who competed drug-free," she said recently. "They should step forward and claim the awards. If I were an American, I would feel cheated."

Carola then provided some insight into her own situation. "When I went to the courtroom and spoke out, I lifted this heavy burden, my sweat clothes that were soaked with guilt and so heavy; they finally came off and I could now get off the blocks," she explained. "This dream has finally ended. For me, testifying and opening the dark box of secrets was my therapy. I can now sleep at night; no more nightmares." When we spoke in January of 2000, Carola laughed. "You know, I had no idea until I came forward, some twenty years after my swimming career, that so many girls were having this same nightmare. We all talked about it at the trial. It's like this curse that was put over the swimming pool. All of us were sharing a piece of the nightmare."

Katrin Meissner, another swimming champion and victim of the GDR system, has relived the trauma. Prior to going to the Berlin courtroom to testify in the Dynamo Swim Club trial, she received threatening phone calls and death threats. She recently gave a radio interview for a Berlin radio station. Shortly before leaving the broadcast, a man called and asked her how she could say such terrible things about the German sports system. Two days later, the same voice left a message on her answering machine, "You will not live long; lock your doors!"

Birgit Heike Matz had been a fifteen-year-old wunderkind. She had cranked out huge training workouts, 400-meter swims eight times in a row at a fast clip. During her court appearance, she insisted that "such a demanding workout would have been impossible without drugs!" While she spoke, the defense attorney and the judge openly remarked on her deep voice and her virile features, mocking the witness.

Birgit Matz was also a victim of the infamous Dr. Binus. But unlike many of the other swimmers of the GDR, she had quite the sense of humor about the subject. She has an engaging style, one that is direct, but not threatening. Now a police inspector in Berlin, Matz comes with some interesting credentials.

Matz began competing at age five, another wunderkind plucked from her youth to go to the special swim house for gifted athletes. Her best accomplishments were winning third place in the 1978 World Championships in the 100-meter and 200-meter backstroke. Then she burned out. She left the pool in 1979 and began her academic career, completing a B.A. and then going on to the elite police academy for special training.

"Even though I am part of a special investigative team, I knew nothing about the indictments of my coach and doctor until I was called by the Berlin prosecutor," said Matz. "I read about some of the indictments, but I was called in to testify and then all the emotions came racing back," she recalled. "I thought I had put this part of my life behind me, but clearly, when the trials began and we faced the defendants, those scumbag doctors, then all the nightmares came flooding in." She sighed.

Matz seemed reticent about giving the next piece of information. After all, as an investigator, she knows something about giving testimony. "I am lucky, I am not suffering from terminal cancer. Perhaps if I had been an Olympic winner, I would not be so fortunate. But I got out early, so I just have lots of embarrassment to deal with," she said. "I have lots of facial hair that I must cover with loads of makeup, my voice is deep, and my liver count is high, but otherwise I'm a healthy woman." Matz is also delightful, a strong woman with a good sense of humor. "I had no problem giving birth; my son is healthy and happy . . . and I am unmarried and . . . living in sin with my man." She laughed.

After Matz testified, her mood was even lighter. "You know, I gave those lawyers a hard time, played with them. "You see, I am a skilled police detective and I know the rules of engagement in the courtroom and how to deal with cross-examinations. I played havoc with the other side. They did not enjoy my testimony!"

Dr. Heukrodt, I Presume

Growing up as the only child of an economist mother and engineer father, Birgit Heukrodt got very special treatment. Aside from the love and nurturance of her parents, she was also given lots of support to be an emerging elite athlete.

Birgit began her illustrious athletic career in 1974 at the SC Dynamo Swim Club in Berlin. It was considered the preeminent club to be part of if you were a rising star, and she was definitely on that trajectory. "At first, I did not have great results, in fact, I didn't make the Olympic team in 1980," she said from her home in Lichetnow, just outside Berlin. "I did start to see some results when I became a student of Rolf Gläser."

Working with Coach Gläser was an honor; it was something you had to earn in the East German system, through respect, obedience, and arduous workouts. Heukrodt fulfilled all of those requirements. She was focused, disciplined, and very determined. "I was the only athlete that he trained for four years, from 1980–1984, and we became very close personal friends," Birgit told me. "It is a relationship that I will cherish but also look back at with some cautious thoughts—there were some very dark moments."

Under the supervision of Gläser and his medical team, Heukrodt started to see some significant progress in her swimming. She trained hard, sometimes six to seven hours a day covering twenty kilometers in the pool, and felt strong and confident. "I started to win big. I took the World and European Championships with several world records in my event," she said with pride. "My memory of this period in my life, with Coach Gläser and with my team, is a joyful one. There were great moments. Because we were training so much and traveling to so many competitions, my coach became a surrogate parent. He was like my father," she said. "I had enormous trust and belief in him, I knew that he would look after me and help me achieve my goals."

Along with the trust and the caring relationship came a blind faith and a routine consumption of "vitamins" in a cup of tea. "We were also given daily injections," she said. "I don't know how I could have been so naive. I never gave any of this a second thought; the pills, the shots, the little things that made such a huge difference in my training. I had such an unconditional trusting and supportive relationship. It never occurred to me that I was being doped."

But after all, her voice became much deeper, and her body took on a new look, with all those sharp, ripped muscles. Yes, and people did notice, and they did comment, but it was all due to the training, she thought. At one point, Heukrodt did ask her trainer and the supervising physician about her body, and they told her that the damp air in the swim pool arena was the cause of these changes. Just an occupational hazard, they said—part of being a world-class swimmer.

In 1984, Heukrodt closed out her athletic career and went to medical school. She devoted that same type of disciplined and focused energy to medicine that she did to swimming, eventually becoming a prominent surgeon. During her early years as a medical student, she began to unlock the big puzzle, the huge secrets of her coach and doctors of the East German swim program. "As a result of my medical studies, I became aware of the effects of anabolic steroids on the body. I remembered my terrible skin condition, the ugly acne scars, and I would ask my team doctor, Dr. Kipke, what that was all about. He said things like, 'You girls, you don't have enough sex, you don't love enough,' referring to the hormonal changes in our bodies," she said with chagrin. "When I think of those times, and my body, I have a deep dark image of this evil man, Kipke. I know from my studies that the injections were causing these changes. He knew that, and he also knew that there would be side effects, long-term consequences. All of the trainers and doctors knew this; it was well-known in the medical literature and has been for many years."

Heukrodt was referring to the Oral-Turinabol, made by VEB Jenapharm, that had already gone through clinical trials. The warning and side-effect labels had been posted in the German PDR (Information for Doctors and Pharmacists Guide), the guidebook used by all medical professionals. It was known in the 1960s that Oral-Turinabol could lead to heart problems, liver dysfunction, and pancreatic distress. As she studied more about medicine and pharmacology, the dark secrets of her past came into full light.

On February 19, 1997, that light turned into a high beam, shedding a full spectrum on Dr. Kipke and the GDR doping machine. That was the opening day of the Berlin doping trials. "This is the date that will remain imprinted in my memory forever," she told me. "This is the date that the doping documents authored by Dr. Kipke came to light. He knew everything: the dosages, the times, the medical thresholds. He had records on everything we did and everything that was injected into our bodies. It was very frightening to see all this in black and white."

Heukrodt acknowledged that the criminal proceedings were terribly painful, stirring up all the suppressed memories and fears. "Now we have to confront all of our past deeds and begin to worry again." Heukrodt was referring to her tumors and other medical problems. She would prefer to tuck it away and move on in her life. "But it is paradoxical," she said. "We need to air this out in the court so that the public will know of the serious damage this has done to us physically and emotionally. Yet there is a part of me that wants to just get on with my life and my career. And there is a part of me that knows German history and how hard change seems to be."

Dr. Lothar Kipke was convicted in January of 2000, receiving a suspended sentence of one year and three months. But by March, just shortly before the new trials set for Ewald and Höppner, the masterminds of GDR doping, Birgit Heukrodt was somewhat cynical about the events over the past two years. "The criminal trials against our trainers and doctors are useful to a point," she allowed, "but they are somewhat superfluous in the big picture. Yes, they have raised the awareness of the public, the German people, but the real issue is that we need to change the attitudes and behavior of all sports-medicine people. We have to get them to shift gears away from this doping mentality," she insisted. "Some will change because of their verdicts and fines, but most sports officials still believe it is okay to use performance-enhancement supplements," she told me.

As a doctor herself, Heukrodt may have some special insights into the mentality of those who supervised her athletic development. She seems keenly aware of the power inherent in their positions. And her point about performance enhancement was a poignant one. If these supplements were universally scorned, doping doctors would be out of business anyway. As the trials of Ewald and Höppner approached, something Dr. Heukrodt had said two years before came into my consciousness. "There is a part of me," she said, "that wants to move on and forget. And there is a part of me that knows the German psyche; these doctors don't really want to change."

At the time, these had sounded like harsh words, perhaps the bitter response of an injured party. But of course, it was hard to say how the doctors would respond to their penalties. After all, none of them would lose their licenses to practice medicine.

19

Guilty Feet Have No Rhythm

The conviction notices filed with the Thirty-fourth Great Criminal Court of the State Court of Berlin in conjunction with case number 534-28-Js-39/97 Kls clearly articulated the criminal actions of trainer Rolf Gläser and swimming team doctor Dr. Dieter Binus, detailing drug usage, time of day, cycles of injections, and performance thresholds. The assertion by Dr. Binus that he had only limited knowledge of the side effects and did not know of harmful long-term reactions to the anabolic steroids was thrown into the garbage pail by the prosecutors. Certified evidence pulled from the STASI files proved that the German scientists employed by VEB Jenapharm knew prior to 1977 about the deadly side effects of their steroid compounds.

The court transcripts were clear:

STATE COURT OF BERLIN in the Name of the People; Criminal Case Defendant 1: Rolf Gläser; Swimming Trainer; Date of birth November 27, 1939, in Dresden, Germany; Residing at Gernlandweg 34, 4060 Leonding,

Austria. Defendant 2: Dr. Dieter Max Werner Binus; Medical Doctor; Date of birth January 11, 1939, in Berlin, Germany; Residing at Königswaelder Strasse 38, 13053 Berlin, Germany.

Charge(s): Willful Bodily Injury. On August 31, 1998, the 34th Great Criminal Court of the State Court of Berlin session has declared that:

- The Defendant Gläser is sentenced for nine counts of Willful Bodily Injury to a fine of 90 (ninety) days wages at DM80 per day.
- The Defendant Dr. Binus is sentenced for two counts of Willful Bodily Injury, as well as for seven counts of Aiding and Abetting Willful Bodily Injury, to a fine of 90 (ninety) days wages at DM100 per day.

The Defendants are directed to pay court costs, their own necessary expenditures, and the necessary expenditures of the Co-Plaintiffs Birgit Matz, Carola Beraktschjan, and Christiane Sommer.

Judge Hansgeorg Bräutigam was a jurist with sterling academic and legal credentials. He was asked to serve on this case not only because of his fairness, but also for his experience with legal process. Born in 1937 in Berlin, Judge Bräutigam had distinguished himself in some very high profile cases. In 1977, he ruled on a series of indictments against terrorists. He was chief jurist in the indictments against President Erich Honecker and other leading GDR officials, including Erich Mielke and Egon Krenz. He also worked as a journalist for many years.

In the doping trials, he had to moderate between the political fallout of East and West and what he considered the true merits of justice. In Bräutigam's view, justice in these cases was based not on the legality of drug use and cheating, but "on the Hippocratic Oath for physicians, which should override any political policy . . . and that oath included not to do harm to anyone, including women and minors."

The ruling began with a concise statement of the matter at hand:

The substance of this proceeding is the accusation against Defendants Dr. Binus and Rolf Gläser, as well as the separated charges against Dr. Bernd Pansold, Volker Frischke, Dieter Krause and Dieter Lindemann, of administering anabolic steroids to nineteen underage female swimmers of the Sport Club SC Dynamo Berlin during the period from 1975 to 1989.

This was followed by an explanation of the decision to separate the cases and then join those of Dr. Binus and Rolf Gläser, and to pursue criminal proceedings against Dr. Binus "only in the cases of witnesses Birgit Heike Matz, Andrea Pinske, Jane Lang, Dr. Birgit Kerstin Heukrodt, Kerstin Olm, Carola Beraktschjan, Heike Meyer, Christiane Sommer, and Marina Mende."

After giving biographies of the defendants, the verdict cut to an outline of a thirty-year master plan to make the GDR the dominant force in international sports. A discussion of Oral-Turinabol stated a central point of the prosecution's case.

The side effects of Oral-Turinabol were listed in the PDR. The guide described in detail the pharmacology and side effects of all Jenapharm products. Dosage guidelines were included as well, and were even shown on the packaging labels. This material was well-known to all GDR doping doctors as far back as 1965. The language was quite straightforward: "the androgenic side effects of anabolics are critical in assessing their scope. They can be unpleasant for women and children. If the treatment with anabolics is long-term, or at high dosages, real possibility for androgenic effects exists. Skin conditions like acne will develop, virilization effects including deepening of voice, growth of facial hair, masculine habits, increased sexual appetite, and clitoris hypertrophy will all occur."

Even among scientists, the side effects of anabolics were well-known. In a journal article published in 1964 in the "newsletter for internal medicine," two leading German scientists, Konrad Eige and Renate Kohler, reported that "androgenic effects can occur in women in the form of virilization, skin changes, and menstrual anomalies."

And so, with the verdicts, the damages followed for co-plaintiffs Heukrodt and Beraktschjan. The court record enumerated the dosages and the number of times they had been given the pills to ingest, showing that the doping had consistently coincided with the approaching competitions.

Dr. Birgit Kerstin Heukrodt, née Meineke:

On a date in the month of January 1980, the then fifteen-year-old witness Birgit Kerstin Heukrodt was transferred into the Training Group of Defendant Gläser at SC Dynamo Berlin. In the time following, Defendant Gläser trained witness Heukrodt at Club level in his so-called A Cadre, as well as at courses of instruction with the National Team Cadre of the GDR and abroad. On an indeterminate date in the fall of the year 1984, but after her participation in the Competition for Friendship in Moscow, the so-called substitute-Olympiad in replacement of the East Bloc boycott of the 1984 Los Angeles Olympiad, witness Heukrodt left the Training Group Gläser for reasons of health and ended her active athletic career.

In the years from 1980 to 1984 witness Heukrodt received from Defendant Gläser, in at least eighteen dispensing cycles of at least 150 mg Oral-Turinabol the following individual doses of the 5 mg blue Oral-Turinabol tablets to ingest:

(CYCLES 1 THROUGH 2)
Because she came to the Training Group Gläser in January 1980, witness Heukrodt received in preparation for the 1980 Moscow Olympic Games beginning in the time frame from January 21 to February 17, 1980, as well as from April 7 to May 19, 1980, from Defendant Gläser over a time frame which lasted three to four weeks in duration, in total at least 150 mg Oral-Turinabol tablets . . . and ingested these tablets.

(CYCLE 3)
In preparation for the European Championships in Yugoslavia in 1981 witness Heukrodt received from Defendant Gläser . . . another round of a total of at least 150 mg Oral-Turinabol tablets . . . and ingested these tablets.

(CYCLE 4 THROUGH 15)

... in the years 1981, 1982, and 1983 ... witness Heukrodt was given ... in respectively four cycles, over a period of respectively three to four weeks per cycle ... a total of at least 600 mg of Oral-Turinabol ... and she ingested these tablets.

This dispensation occurred in accordance with the UM-Concept because witness Heukrodt took part in the European Championships in Yugoslavia in 1981, was preparing for World Championships in Ecuador in 1982, participated in these World Championships in the summer of 1982, prepared from the fall of 1982 for the European Championships in Rome to be held in the summer of 1983, and then participated in that competition. In the fall of 1983 preparations began for the Olympiad in Los Angeles in the summer of 1984, so that the 4th (fourth) dispensing cycle of the Oral-Turinabol tablets closed the calendar year 1983.

(CYCLES 16 THROUGH 18)

In further preparation for the year's high point of 1984, the Competition for Friendship in Moscow, the so-called substitute-Olympiad in replacement of the East Bloc boycott of the 1984 Los Angeles Olympiad, witness Heukrodt ... received from Defendant Gläser in total at least 150 mg Oral-Turinabol ... and ingested these tablets.

Carola Beraktschjan, née Nitschke

On a date in September of 1975 ... the then-thirteen-year-old witness Carola Beraktschjan was transferred into the Training Group of Defendant Gläser at SC

Dynamo Berlin. In the time following, Defendant Gläser trained witness Beraktschjan at Club level in his so-called A Cadre, as well as at courses of instruction with the National Team Cadre of the GDR and abroad. In the year 1979 . . . witness Beraktschjan left the Training Group Gläser because of a disagreement concerning the dispensing of tablets and injections, and returned to the Training Group Hoffmann, before she finally ended her active athletic career in the year 1980.

The witness Beraktschjan, before the 1976 Olympiad and then until 1977, received from Defendant Gläser, in at least 5 (five) dispensing cycles of at least 150 mg Oral-Turinabol . . .

(CYCLE 1)
In preparation for the 1976 Montreal Olympic Games, witness Beraktschjan received from Defendant Gläser . . . in total at least 150 mg Oral-Turinabol tablets . . . and ingested these tablets.

(CYCLE 2)
In preparation for the European Championships in Sweden 1977 witness Beraktschjan received from Defendant Gläser . . . a total of at least 150 mg Oral-Turinabol tablets . . . and ingested these tablets.

(CYCLES 3 TO 5)
In further preparation for the European Championships in Sweden 1977 witness Beraktschjan received from Defendant Gläser . . . from January/February 1977 and from March to May 1977 a total of at least 150 mg Oral-Turinabol tablets . . . and ingested these tablets.

The witness Beraktschjan did participate in the European Championships in 1977.

During her time with Training Group Gläser the Defendant Dr. Binus administered to witness Beraktschjan on an indeterminate date in the time before her participation in the European Championships in Sweden in 1977 an intramuscular injection of Depot-Turinabol, and thereby with at least 50 mg of Nandrolone decanoate. In accordance with the knowledge at that time in the GDR concerning the dissipation rate for Depot-preparations and the prescribed guidelines for their use, at least 30 (thirty) days must remain between the last application and the competition, or the test, so that the injection with Depot-Turinabol must have been injected in a time frame from as much as 30 (thirty) days prior to the European Championships, or the first competition.

The Defendant Dr. Binus performed this injection, although he knew that the injection was not medically indicated, and that the administered dose of Nandrolone decanoate would significantly affect the hormonal regulation of the witness Beraktschjan, as well as significantly endanger her health. The defendant Dr. Binus defends himself with 'hands and feet,' as the witness wants to read the label on the ampule.

In regard to liver tumors and other liver damage, the expert witnesses emphasized that the concurrent administration of Oral-Turinabol and 'the Pill' represents a significant increase in the risk of such liver damage, because both medications contain the so-called 17-a-alkyl steroids, which trigger these damages. The risk is further increased based on the dosage and the duration of taking these alkyl steroids. . . . It is plausible that the elevated liver enzyme levels found in the medical records of witnesses Beraktschjan and Matz are attributable to repetitive doses of anabolic steroids. . . . The diagnosis in witness Dr. Heukrodt in November 1993 of focal nodular hyperplasia, a very rare, benign liver tumor was probably initiated by many years of taking 'the Pill,' and to an approximately equally long period, even preceding 'the Pill,' of taking anabolic steroids (overlap period: six (6) months). After stopping the medication the tumor shrank from a diameter of ten (1) CM down to a diameter of three point five (3.5) CM.

In summary, a reading of the depositions provided to the main hearing shows that of five (5) of nine (9) or eleven (11) female swimmers examined—the witnesses Beraktschjan, Matz, Olm, Sommer and Dr. Heukrodt—experienced a partially reversible deepening of the voice incurred as a probable result of anabolics; that one (1) of the swimmers—witness Matz—experienced facial hair growth that was very probably caused or exacerbated by the anabolics; that two (2) of the swimmers—witnesses Matz and Beraktschjan—experienced moderate liver damage (elevated transaminasen levels), that is probably attributable to the effects of anabolics; that one (1) of the female swimmers—witness Dr. Heukrodt—was found to have a liver tumor after eight (8) years of taking 'the Pill' and an approximately equivalent period of taking anabolics. The involvement of anabolics in these circumstances is viewed as 'probable' from a medical standpoint.

When Judge Bräutigam discussed the case by telephone in early April 2000 from his home outside Berlin, he was passionate about his role in the early GDR doping trials. "This was not so much about drugs, the Olympics, and performance enhancement," he said thoughtfully. "This was more a legal case about doing harm to innocent minors, children, if you will, who were given pills and injections against their will and without informed consent. This is the essence of the crime," he explained, "and the legal precedent was set because it was a conviction against perpetrators from a previous government that no longer exists."

20

Supreme Court Speaks the Truth

On February 10, 2000, Professor Werner Franke called to inform me that a fax was on its way over the international wires. He sounded more upbeat than usual; he seemed rather cheerful, and his voice reflected a sense of calm. "We have won a major battle," he shouted over the phone line. "Brigitte and I feel very happy about the original verdict by Judge Bräutigam. The Supreme Court of Germany has upheld the lower verdicts!"

Indeed, the day before, the Fifth District of the German Supreme Court (Bundesgerichtshof), had denied the appeal of Dr. Bernd Pansold and his colleagues and let stand the 180-day sentence and large deutsche mark fine imposed on the GDR doctors for causing bodily harm in nine doping cases.

It was cause for major celebration for Berendonk and Franke, who had waged a twenty-five-year battle to expose the GDR doping machine. The Supreme Court refused to overturn the original verdict from the lower court, citing the fact that the statute of limitations had not run on this case with the former East German government and that these "crimes had not been prosecuted in the GDR." The court was incensed, and in its opinion cited the nine athletes and their medical problems associated with being doped. They also pointed out that eight of the nine elite athletes were minors; seven of them between the ages of thirteen and sixteen. The court noted that their "parents had been lied to and that the drugs were removed from their original packages and disguised as vitamins."

It was a huge win for Franke and Berendonk and an even bigger vindication for athletes Christiane Knacke-Sommer and Carola Beraktschjan, who had filed cross appeals in the case. It was also a statement from the prosecutors and the new German government that this was not just politics as usual, but in fact crimes against humanity, and teenage humanity as well.

Judge Bräutigam had expected the ruling, too, but was equally delighted with the overall outcome. "Yes, the Supreme Court supported my earlier decision," he said shortly after learning of the decision. "But more important, they also established some legal precedent for other officials—high-ranking ones—to be indicted and perhaps convicted of these awful crimes against minors," he said with satisfaction. "We were not sure how they would rule on the statute of limitations, but we did have some precedent here with the shootings at the Berlin Wall, so I was confident they would rule in our favor."

As Bräutigam confirmed, this was not an easy case in the beginning. A wall of silence had been erected when prosecutors went to investigate the doping crimes. "It was very hard to get people to talk, both perpetrators and victims," he explained with some hesitation. "I was not sure why we had so much silence—perhaps fear, perhaps emotional trauma—but no one would talk. So it was the STASI file, the archives, that actually broke through this wall. They spoke volumes. Every minute detail, with every athlete attached to each detail, was in the file, so we used this as our road map as we weaved our way through the legal process. After we had possession of the documents, people finally came forward to talk."

Mindful of the complexities of the case, Bräutigam was circumspect in his responses about the convictions and the verdicts in these crimes against humanity. When asked why the sentences were relatively light, he said, "You must understand that these doping cases were tried under a new government with new laws, all new legal territory, so we were treading on delicate judicial ground. These were crimes committed under a different social, political, and legal background in the old GDR, so we had to apply our statutes—and in some cases waive the statute of limitations—to apply appropriate law. We also knew that like similar political crimes from the East, we would offer lighter sentences for the corporals, and hand down heavier ones for the generals," he said, referring to the masterminds of the GDR doping plan.

Bräutigam was forthcoming and, in fact, quite insightful when speaking of the victims. "I found that many of the athletes, especially the older women, were very open and extremely helpful in giving us testimony about the pills, the injections, the abuse they encountered at their training sites. But many of the younger athletes were reticent, fearful and intimidated by the process. Perhaps they were in a permanent state of denial," he offered. "I'm not exactly sure how to describe this, but some athletes who testified in my court were just emotionally closed; they did not remember anything, almost like a temporary amnesia."

Bräutigam seemed to have a marked sensitivity for the athletes, as if he knew them well. He exhibited a great deal of compassion for their situation. It had an intimacy that he apparently understood and could participate in.

"At one point in the proceedings we had to ask the women some very delicate questions about their medical histories, their physiology, their female anatomy. In fact, we hired expert gynecologists to do examinations to determine the effects of the steroids on their bodies. It was very detailed and very personal," he recalled. "And so, I felt this collective pain and trauma in my courtroom, and on many days we removed the media, the spectators, the other witnesses, to reduce the embarrassment, the trauma to the women testifying. It was very painful at times. I witnessed many upsetting moments in my court," he noted respectfully. "For example, the witness, Birgit Heukrodt, was very forthcoming, very articulate, and willing to disclose all of the doping details. She was a very big asset to the case, as were others.

"Others, however, wanted to recant their testimony and deny their earlier statements to prosecutors, so we had a lot of difficulty at times getting a clear picture. I believe many of the athletes were reliving the trauma of their swimming days in the GDR," he suggested, "and it was overwhelming. Others were willing to go through the experience and, I believe, came through with some sense of closure."

The five-judge panel—Judges Harris, Nack, Häger, Gerhardt, and Basdorf—noted in their decision that there were other cases where the statute had been waived in crimes of the former GDR. They cited the shootings at the Berlin Wall, the kidnapping of GDR citizens, public humiliation of Germans, and now doping. For the Franke-Lehner legal team, it was nothing less than a triumph and a very big win.

The judges were infuriated by the fact that "it was a state-run program, top-secret, and serious bodily harm was committed." In addition, the judges articulated the fact that the crimes were serious, as athletes were used as "instruments of the state, just victims manipulated by the system."

This decision came on the heels of another unprecedented legal ruling in Germany. In September 1998, a new law was passed that allowed for ten-year prison sentences for anyone dispensing anabolic steroids to minors.

Bräutigam viewed these developments as pure justice. "I was not there to preside over International Olympic doping rules, or make judgments about individuals who use drugs in sport. That is not my role. I simply wanted to set the record straight and set legal precedent for those who had committed crimes against minors, for those doctors who had abused their Hippocratic privilege and manipulated the bodies of youngsters and to be sure that we never have this happen again. This was my role," he said modestly. "It is my hope that perhaps, in addition to the legal standard, we all set a new moral standard that other countries might look at."

A final notation was made at the bottom of the German Supreme Court decision. It said: "The fact that doping is widespread in many countries is irrelevant in the case at hand."

I Am Technik

At the time of the Supreme Court decision, Ute Krause was preparing to testify at the upcoming Höppner and Ewald trial in Berlin. However, her moment of truth had come many years earlier, in 1983—with a suicide attempt.

One of the fastest 200-meter backstroke swimmers in the world going into the 1980 Olympics in Moscow, Krause dropped out of the athletic arena in the late 1970s due to a severe eating disorder and clinical depression. "It was just one small stone in the mosaic of my life," she said. At the time, Krause could not make any sense of her feelings. She attributed her extreme weight fluctuations to her swimming and the stress of training. But she could not figure out her emotional swings and her deep depression. "I just had no clue what was going on," she said recently. Every time I mentioned my problems to a coach, he would say not to worry, 'keep training and keep swallowing the vitamins. You will get stronger and better.' "

"I had no idea what was happening to me," she continued. "I would be anorexic one minute, bulimic the next—it was crazy. Then I got seriously depressed. I had no one to turn to, not even my parents. I didn't trust anyone. I was scared of doctors, coaches, trainers—everyone. So I took some powerful medications and drank myself unconscious. I woke up in a pool of vomit, not knowing if I was dead or alive. . . . Then I knew it was time to get help."

After retiring from swimming, Krause went to work in a nursing home. Then, in 1984, came the next "stone" in her life's mosaic. One day she looked in on a patient as part of her routine and noticed some blue and pink pills on the elderly woman's night table. They were Oral-Turinabol tabs—the same size, colors, and dosage as those she had been swallowing for years at the pool. She was shocked. For the first time, she saw the box and medical instructions for ingestion. As she read the pharmaceutical insert, she became perplexed. "These were steroids, not vitamins," she realized.

She immediately went to the supervising physician. "He explained that these pills, the Oral-Turinabol, were prescribed for cancer patients to build their immune system while chemo and radiation were used during their treatment." Recalling from her job application that Krause had been an elite athlete in the GDR's program, the doctor told her "the big secret—these drugs were meant to build us up and make us huge and allow us to recover rapidly. It was ghastly. I was so horrified," she said.

Krause's reaction went from shock to disbelief. "How could these doctors and trainers do this to me? I was suffering from an eating disorder, then my depression, then my suicide attempt, and no one told me why. . . . How cruel," she moaned.

Eventually, her disbelief turned to outrage. By the time she was approached by federal prosecutors in early 2000, she was eager to testify.

On May 2, 2000, Manfred Höppner, the chief of the GDR doping program, was brought to a courthouse in downtown Berlin. Because of the throng of reporters jamming the entrance, the proceedings started late. Television crews from around the world, including ABC's *20/20,* were jockeying for position to see the big event.

Judge Dirk Dickhaus had stepped in at the last minute, appointed by the federal bench after Judge Walter Neuhaus had apparently become too ill to hear the case. Höppner was escorted into the courtroom through a side door, sealed off by heavy security. Seated before Judge Dickhaus, Höppner listened as he was charged with orchestrating the biggest doping scam in the history of modern sport.

Prosecutor Klaus Heinrich Debes read the indictment in a monotone: "You are charged with causing bodily harm to 142 women." Rica Reinisch, Karen König, Martina Gottschalt, Ute Krause, Jutta Gottschalk, Birgit Matz, Carola Nitschke-Beraktschjan, Birgit Meineke Heukrodt, Kornelia Otto, Kornelia Ender Gummt, Andreas Krieger, Michael Droese, Margitta Pufe, Barbara Krause, Petra Kind Schneider, Christiane Knacke-Sommer, Catherine Menschner, Kathleen Nord, Ines Geipel, Birgit Paist Boese, Yvonne Stierwald Bebhardt, Simone Michel Machalett, Brigitte Sander Michel, Martina Opitz Hellman, and Marita Koch were all present, listening intently as the government stated its case. They were all prepared for this, the last trial.

Dr. Manfred Höppner was born in 1934, in the city of Meissen. In his youth, he was a successful track and field athlete. After attending medical school, he moved into the area of elite sports medicine. There he recognized opportunity. While working part-time for the STASI police, he moved his way up the sports-medicine hierarchy. From 1966 on, he had his finger on the pulse of all performance-enhancement activity in GDR sports.

Höppner got his start on the international scene when he accompanied the East German Olympic Team to Mexico City in 1968. He took personal responsibility for his athletes in those days. In fact, Höppner had sole credit for the first GDR doping success.

Margitta Gummel was a nationally ranked shot-putter. She became Höppner's star pupil. After a regimen of doping organized by Höppner, Gummel set a world record in the shot and threw an unprecedented 19.61 meters, beating out all of the others by long yards, and thus becoming the first "official" success of GDR doping. Her competitors, including Brigitte Berendonk, knew that she was full of something. "She was huge," Berendonk recalled. "She had massive shoulders and arms. Her body had transformed since the last time we competed. She was clearly a she-man."

Höppner was so successful that East Germany's Olympic take went from twenty gold medals in 1972 to an astounding forty at the 1976 Olympics, where women won eleven of thirteen events in swimming. (In 1977, as Debes noted in his prepared statement at the trial, Höppner warned his superior, Ewald, "not to let any female athletes do television interviews," referring to their deepened voices.)

According to Höppner, for most of his professional life he

operated with a "split personality," a dichotomy that, he says, now haunts him. On the one hand, he organized and administered the whole GDR doping system, working with high-level government officials, the pharmaceutical labs, and the sports-medicine doctors. In the other aspect of his psyche, he professed to all his colleagues that he promoted clean sport. He was even a member of the prestigious Physicians Commission of the World Track and Field Organization, a group under the umbrella of the IOC. He told one reporter that after the unification of Germany in 1991, "this double standard was very stressful for me and caused me great internal conflict."

Judge Dickhaus gave Höppner five minutes to make an opening statement. "Competitive sport and sport for health are absolutely different things," Höppner began. Citing the renowned author Bertolt Brecht, he declared, "Competitive sport begins where healthy sport ends." He proceeded with a rationale of his actions. "Many people pop pills in order to maintain their ability to work hard, so where is the real difference between sport and the real world? Doctors in the sports-medicine field don't have the opportunity to certify an athlete unfit for work, but the athletes nevertheless ask the doctors to help them maintain their competitive edge. So doctors should not shy away from this question. It is always like walking a tightrope."

The courtroom was packed. Sitting in a cordoned-off area, protected by two armed guards, were the athlete/coplaintiffs, quietly observing the proceedings. As Höppner went on, their faces took on looks of astonishment.

"According to the 1987 pharmaceutical law," he continued, "the proper use of drugs includes the prevention of damage. We did scientific studies in the East to prove that it was necessary to use these supporting means, these drugs, for performance. We justified our use of the drugs to prevent damage to the athletes," he claimed. "Even today we have an ongoing discussion about the ethics of using performance enhancement," he said, looking at the judge. "If the court finds that I am wrong about the use of drugs, then I have to accept this, but twenty-six years ago, the situation was very different. The objective of supplying these pills was to minimize injury and maximize training hours."

By this time, the athletes who had come to the criminal courthouse to bear witness and testify appeared to be in a state of shock.

Höppner compared the use of anabolics to the consumption of alcohol and tobacco, noting that the latter are not prohibited but have severe health consequences. He then delivered a huge slap in the face to those seated in the Berlin courtroom. "I did not want our athletes to end up dead like Ms. Dressel," he said, making a reference to the West German track star who apparently died of complications associated with steroids.

Turning to his codefendant, Höppner then made his closing remarks. "In 1988, there was severe pressure to start using human growth hormone to boost performance. But I thought it was dangerous, so I rejected the idea and even tried to change jobs. I applied for a hospital job, but," he said, looking at Ewald, "my superior would not permit it. He would not let me go. He was very influential in the East and could have harmed my career."

Ewald shifted nervously in his seat.

At this point the judge interrupted and asked Höppner if

he had personally administered steroids. Höppner acknowledged that he had done so. As the session came to a close, Michael Lehner's assistant, Mr. Mohr, asked that the court note that "Mr. Höppner not only assisted with steroid use but was actively engaged in causing bodily harm." The motion was accepted and noted for the record.

An important distinction had been drawn—one that could have severe consequences when sentences were announced.

A few hours after the day's court session, Rica Reinisch commented on Höppner's court debut. "He made statements that were insane. He made us look like fools. He admits on the one hand that he gave us drugs, but then he says he did it in the name of health and prevention, to protect us from hurting ourselves. He is out of his mind."

Prior to the start of the May 8 court session, Frank Osterloh approached the judge's bench. His client, Manfred Ewald, seventy-four years old, was, according to his attorney, not in good health. Stating for the record that "Mr. Ewald was not able to hear the indictments and was too sick to understand their ramifications," Osterloh petitioned the court for a recess so that Mr. Ewald could be examined by a physician and a psychiatrist to determine whether he was healthy enough to stand trial.

Like his employee, Höppner, Manfred Ewald also took on multiple roles. Born in 1926, the son of a tailor, Ewald joined the Hitler Youth in 1938. By age fourteen he had quit school and started a job in Stettin. He wanted to be a government administrator. In 1942, at the age of sixteen, Ewald infiltrated the resistance movement, posing as a communist. He was actually an up-and-coming aspirant in the Nazi order, and in 1944 he became a member of the National Socialist, or Nazi, party.

At an early age, Ewald learned how to operate in two distinct worlds. Walter Ulbricht, a leading political figure in the East, named Ewald secretary of state for sport when he was only twenty-six years old. Later, he studied in Moscow, learning the ins and outs of the Communist Party. His early success led to his prestigious appointment as the president of the National Olympic Committee for all of GDR sports. A member of the Central Committee of the GDR by the age of twenty-seven, he was established as a serious power broker in all aspects of politics and sport.

Whereas Höppner admitted to giving steroids and made partial apologies in the name of health and well-being, Ewald had been stone-cold silent. In fact, when first subpoenaed to testify in the doping trials, he proclaimed, "Communists do not murder people. We had no involvement in this matter whatsoever."

Carola Beraktschjan, thirty-eight, testified on that day. During her testimony, Judge Dickhaus interrupted and asked for clarification on a few technical points.

JUDGE: Which drugs were given to you and in what form?

BERAKTSCHJAN: When I began, at age eleven, I got a few pills. As I got older, I was given more and more; up to thirty pills a day.

JUDGE: Did you know what they were?

BERAKTSCHJAN: At first they were in wrappers, but as I got older the color changed and they had no markings or package.

JUDGE: What was the color?

BERAKTSCHJAN: They were little blue ones.

JUDGE: Did you get injections?

BERAKTSCHJAN: Yes, in my buttocks. Dr. Binus injected me, and he got angry when I asked to see the label. I gained lots of weight—20 kg that year.

JUDGE: How did the doctors explain your very deep voice and your changes?

BERAKTSCHJAN: They told me to swim and not sing.

Ute Krause testified that day, too. "In the courtroom," she said afterward, "I was nervous and insecure, but I managed to find the confidence to confront Dr. Höppner and Ewald, and tell them both, looking them straight in their eyes, that they were evil and they hurt me. I told them how I threw up all the time, then how I binged with my eating. Then I told them how I hated myself, how I felt like a big barrel in the pool and how I wanted to get help, and I felt helpless. I told them I wanted to kill myself, and I tried."

The support of the other athletes, she said, gave her strength. "I got up and told these men how they shattered my life. And for a brief moment, I saw fear and anxiety in their eyes. . . . This gave me a sense of power and confidence, and for the first time in my life I did not feel like a victim."

Rica Reinisch was asked to return to the courtroom to testify on May 10. As one of the coplaintiffs, a well-respected

1980 Olympic medalist and public-television commentator, she was asked to coordinate efforts among other athletes and to be a lead witness in the Ewald and Höppner trials.

The prosecutor questioned her about her "supportive means" and doping protocols. "I got out of the pool, went to see my coach, and then he gave me some blue pills in a chocolate box," Reinisch testified. "When I asked my coach what they were for, he said, They are 'aufbauende mittel' . . . they will build you up, they are good for you, just swallow them."

Reinisch was asked about the impact of the steroids and her medical problems. "My coach took me directly from Moscow to a clinic in Dresden, where I was examined by Dr. Loffler, who treated me for a serious stomach ailment," she told the prosecutor. "He explained to me for the first time what the drugs were doing to me—my voice, the appalling acne all over my neck and shoulders, and now my stomach infections. I tried to quit swimming, but Dr. Röder, the swim doc, came to see me to convince me to return to the pool. He said I was the best backstroker in the world (at that point), and he said I needed to swim for the GDR."

When it came time for cross-examination, Mildebrandt, the defense attorney, proceeded to ask Reinisch the same questions he had asked the other coplaintiffs.

MILDEBRANDT: Didn't you know what the pills were for?
REINISCH: No.
MILDEBRANDT: Didn't you talk amongst yourselves?
REINISCH: We weren't allowed to.
MILDEBRANDT: Did you talk to your parents?
REINISCH: We were told not to discuss anything.

MILDEBRANDT: Were you told to be quiet?

REINISCH: Yes.

MILDEBRANDT: Did you ask your doctor?

REINISCH: He wouldn't speak to me about this. We weren't allowed to talk to anyone.

Reinisch was disturbed not only by the series of questions, but by the demeanor of the defendants—"They just sat there looking feeble and stupid, especially Ewald"—and by the facetious and condescending tone of the defense lawyers. It was bad enough, she said, just to have to talk about the side effects. "The prosecutor asked about my body and physical changes and I told him I had huge muscles and that my voice changed, and that my music teacher said it was unbelievable how deep my voice became; it was humiliating." To have the defense attorneys waving their hands in disdain and treating the whole matter as if these "girls" shouldn't be wasting the time of the court was just too much to bear. "They were acting like this was a charade," said Reinisch.

At one point, Reinisch said, she was so upset she had to leave the courtroom. She pulled herself together and then came back to resume her testimony. "I felt that the judge was very sympathetic, and he knew I was struggling to get through my statements.

"I had prepared myself for the trials. I had rehearsed my testimony and knew what I needed to say. But I did get very emotional, and it was difficult to control myself at times," she admitted. When the defense attorney suggested that her medical problems were all a thing of the past, that the whole matter was inconsequential and did not merit the attention of the public, she exploded. "You don't seem to be understanding it. I live with pain constantly," she cried out in the courtroom. "I have inflammations of my ovaries, I have had two miscarriages, and I am required to take beta-blockers for my heart arrhythmia. I live daily with pain. You don't get it!"

Reinisch was livid. "I was so outraged at the behavior of the attorneys for Ewald and Höppner," she said. "They didn't realize that many of us were fighting for our lives."

May 16, the fourth session of the criminal trial of Ewald and Höppner, was the occasion for several developments. Judge Dickhaus began the proceedings by stating that Ewald had been examined and two medical opinions had rendered him fit to stand trial—but for only two hours each session.

In a surprise attempt to mask the serious nature of steroid use and distance himself further from Ewald, Höppner made a statement that appeared to shock even the judge. "We did give anabolic steroids to certain women along with vitamin D to cure Scheuerman's disease," a reference to a neurological disorder.

On the same day, Höppner's attorney, Hans Peter Milde-brandt, stated for the record that athletes attending the previous sessions had threatened Mr. Höppner, saying things such as "I want to smash his face in," suggesting that there was intimidation by the coplaintiffs.

The close of the day's session provided one of the lighter moments. A statement was read by the prosecutor, referring to Höppner's "active involvement" in every aspect of sport. In March 1984, while in Karl-Marx-Stadt for an international athletic competition, Höppner was responsible for checking urine samples for drug use. He knew that certain weight lifters were using steroids and that the Kreischa lab would find them to be positive tests. So he ran to the bathroom, broke open the seals of the urine specimen bottles, poured out the contents, and took a nice long leak of pure urine into them. He then reported to his chief, Manfred Ewald, that all of the urine tests (and athletes) were drug-free.

During the next proceeding, on May 26, Karen König had her second chance in court. She had testified earlier in the Sünder and Rösler case. Today it was her turn to give a prepared statement. Afterward, she, too, was questioned by the judge.

JUDGE: When did you get the pills?

KÖNIG: Since 1979, I got a few blue ones, and then later eight to ten pills a day of other colors.

JUDGE: Did you know what they were?

KÖNIG: No, but I was suspicious. My parents had to sign a statement of secrecy, that they could not talk about my swim program with anyone.

JUDGE: Did you have effects?

KÖNIG: Yes, I got terribly depressed and I went to get counseling.

JUDGE: Did you talk to anyone?

KÖNIG: We were not allowed to talk to anyone. It was against the rules.

Other athletes were given permission to make statements as well. The list was long. And even now, as the publicity for the trial had increased, more athletes, fearful that they would not be included in the record as having been victimized by the GDR doping system, were coming forward.

That same day, the court heard Heike Rödiger Grünler, a tall, attractive blonde who started swimming at the age of four. Rising quickly in the ranks, she became the European champion in 1982.

JUDGE: When did you start getting the pills?

GRÜNLER: I got the pills, the blue ones, from the fourth grade on. The doctors told me to eat them, to swallow, not to throw them away.

JUDGE: What were your problems?

GRÜNLER: I became very sick. I fainted often, I had seizures, terrible menstrual cramps, and I put on lots of weight.

JUDGE: What else changed?

GRÜNLER: My parents noticed my voice changing, but my muscles did not grow very large, so the doctors were disappointed with my results.

And then, on May 30, came Andreas Krieger, formerly known as Heidi, now a man after a long and stressful struggle with his identity as a woman and as a successful female Olympian. Krieger had been one of the world's preeminent shot-putters and discus throwers. He had a host of world championships under his belt, with throws in both events that were beyond twenty-one meters (in the shot) and sixty meters in the discus, distances that were considered impossible without the use of steroids.

He came to court with a prepared statement. His hair was cut short and he was dressed in jeans and cowboy boots. He stood up and faced the two defendants directly.

JUDGE: When did you get your drugs?

KRIEGER: In 1983, I got the blue ones but also got birth-control pills as well.

At this point Krieger moved to the bench and handed the judge a wrinkled piece of paper. "I would like you to see what I looked like as a girl, Your Honor. This is before the drugs, the injections, the violations, and then my confusion, which led to my sex change." Judge Dickhaus looked puzzled, yet intrigued. He nodded as Krieger returned to the witness box.

JUDGE: How did you know things were changing?

KRIEGER: Dr. Wendler gave me these pills, and I had fevers and chills and had terrible cramps.

JUDGE: What was the worst part of your illness?

KRIEGER: I was hospitalized in 1987, and Dr. Wendler came to the room and told me to get ready, I needed to prepare for my next competition. They just used me like a machine.

JUDGE: When did you feel the changes take place in your body?

KRIEGER: I could not go out in public. I did not feel like a woman. I hid from everyone. I hated my body, and my mind was crazy with panic.

JUDGE: Then what?

KRIEGER: I became suicidal, and I went to several doctors to ask if I could change from being a woman to being a man. I could not live within this body any longer.

JUDGE: It seems that you were struggling emotionally and physically. Did you get help?

KRIEGER: Yes, in 1997. I crossed over. I went to a specialist and had my breasts removed, a hysterectomy, and some other surgical procedures, so that I am now a man.

JUDGE: Are you better today?

KRIEGER: I still get depressed; I'm unemployed. But my mother has been a great support to me. She says no matter who I am, boy or girl, she will always love me.

JUDGE: Do you know the defendants Höppner and Ewald?

KRIEGER: In fact, I do. I was in Leningrad on a study tour with other athletes and Dr. Höppner was there. I think he knew me well, and he had my files destroyed so nobody would know the seriousness of my illness.

May 30 was also the day that Ines Giepel, who had been a world-class sprinter, testified. As were many other witnesses before her, she was asked the questions: How did you know these were drugs? Why didn't you ask? Didn't your parents know? You must have known . . . why didn't you refuse? Again and again, she had heard the defense lawyers mocking the witnesses, grimacing at their answers, exchanging glances that seemed to belittle their suffering.

Giepel, a journalist and specialist in German studies with several published books to her credit, asked the judge for permission to speak. Once permission was granted, she made known her outrage at the way she and the other witnesses were being denigrated, as women as well as athletes. She denounced Mildebrandt for his impertinent manner of asking the same questions over and over, accusing him of treating the athletes like abused children—and in effect, abusing them again. Referring to the witnesses as Mauerkinder—"children of the wall"—she decried the way the defense was inflicting further pain on those who had already endured so much.

The crowd in the courtroom shouted out in support of her statement. All of the athlete/coplaintiffs stood up and applauded. So great was the tumult that Judge Dickhaus threatened to clear the courtroom if there was another such outburst. It was not the place of the spectators to raise their voices in support, he said. It was his courtroom. And he would not permit abuse in his courtroom, he insisted.

With that, the judge called the day's session to an end.

As of June 16, 2000, the trial was still in progress. With the intense publicity surrounding the trial and the knowledge that the statute of limitations would soon run out, many more witnesses were due to appear before the federal prosecutor and Judge Dickhaus. These athlete/victims would no doubt have chilling stories to tell about their lives as child prodigies and superstar athletes of the great GDR. They would also tell the stories of their bewildered families, their deformed children, their fights with depression and suicide, and how they have coped with a twenty-five-year nightmare.

Shortly after her court appearance, Rica Reinisch expressed great disappointment in her fellow athletes. "There are so many victims and so many people who are just scared and intimidated; they won't come forward. There are many mothers who gave birth to deformed children and they are afraid to come out of hiding, afraid that their lives will be shattered further." She admitted that she was bitter about this. "We took risks to get to court, to indict these criminals. We put our lives and our professions on the line. And yet many victims will not be heard," she said sadly. "Justice will not be served in full measure."

A single mother raising two healthy children, with a good job working for public television, Reinisch considers herself one of the lucky ones. "But my fellow athletes are suffering. Many are very depressed, can't hold a job. And most are broke, they don't have a deutsche mark to their name. Their lives are shattered."

Reinisch has other worries. She feels that the public is not well informed. The trials were just the tip of the iceberg, she claims. "We still have a lab at Kreischa that is experimenting with doping substances; we still today, in June 2000, have kids who are on performance-enhancement drugs. . . . Will it ever end?"

Coors Country

When Werner Franke got off the plane in Denver on a cold fall Rocky Mountain day, his greatest fear, he said, was not the weather, but having to drink some beer that might not be on a par with the great German brews.

It was October of 1998, around the time when the GDR doping trials were just getting under way. Werner Franke had come to Colorado Springs for a series of meetings with some key players in the sports world. Aside from his plans to meet with the governor and share a few beers with the president of Coors, Professor Franke was on a special mission. He had come to Colorado for a candid discussion with Bill Hybl, USOC president, and Richard Young, the chief counsel for U.S. swimming, about the fact that doping is pervasive, not only in Germany, but throughout the world.

"I don't have to convince the Americans that they have problems," he acknowledged privately when he arrived. "They know that there is EPO, HgH, blood doping, and steroid use across the spectrum," he said in his most diplomatic tone. But he was irritated by all the finger-pointing at the Germans because of the GDR doping scandal. He knew that while the best and the brightest of the Olympic doping experts resided in Germany, there were some culprits in other countries who seemed to have made their mark, too.

"Essentially, I told Bill Hybl and Richard Young and the governor that the Americans need to clean the skeletons from their closet as well," he reported after his meetings with them. "You folks are wimps, because nobody is willing to take on the IOC and their drug testing and their corrupt lab practices. Doping is not systematic in the States and was never organized as a state plan, [as in] the GDR, but you have pockets of individuals who are well trained in beating the Olympic drug tests," he asserted.

Franke's mini-lecture was received with polite nods by our top sports officials. "I'm not sure they wanted to hear my ranting and raving"—he laughed—"but I let them know my intent. I like to shoot straight with everyone, regardless of their credentials."

Franke had also come to the States to offer some moral support to the U.S. legal team and their clients, the American athletes who had witnessed their competitors beating them up big-time, knowing full well their bodies were chemically engineered.

Attorney Richard Young had recently petitioned the IOC to get the record book corrected for American Olympians who had been cheated out of medals because of the GDR's scheme. Young, who represented the U.S. Swimming Federation, had filed an informal affidavit with the IOC asking that the Americans who had placed behind the East German women in Olympic events where doping was present be reinstated. He did not want to take medals away from German athletes; he had petitioned for the

American swimmers' right to simply be acknowledged as winners along with their German competitors.

The strategy was meant to appeal to global fairness—not intending to victimize anyone (including the German swimmers who were already suffering), but only to recognize the accomplishments of American swimmers who had competed drug-free.

Young and Franke shared the view that it seemed only ethical to promote this co-medal acknowledgment. They asked that international Olympic officials note for the record that there were multiple gold medalists at the 1976 Montreal Olympics in swimming. For example, in the 100-meter freestyle, Kornelia Ender of the GDR won a gold medal in a world-record time of 55.65 seconds. She was followed by teammate Petra Priemer at 56.49 for the silver and Enith Brigitha of Holland at 56.65 for the bronze. Kim Payton of the United States took fourth in 56.81, but under this plan would move up two slots as a co-medalist and share the silver. In the 200-meter freestyle, GDR superstar Kornelia Ender won gold in 1:59:26 for another world record, followed by Shirley Babashoff from the United States in 2:01:22. Babashoff, who has been very outspoken about the injustice of German doping, would share co–gold medal status with Ms. Ender. In the 400-meter freestyle, also in Montreal, Petra Thümer of the GDR won gold and set a new world record in 4:09:89, while Babashoff finished second in a time of 4:10:46. In short, in this scenario, more athletes would share the wealth.

Montreal seemed to be the benchmark for performance-enhanced success by the East German swim team. In the 800-meter freestyle, Petra Thümer set a world record and won gold in 8:37:14, followed by Babashoff (who took and

CHANGING SILVER INTO GOLD

The 1976 Olympics women's swimming competition is one of the biggest sources of controversy involving possible East German drug use.

100-METER FREE

	1976	Review
Kornelia Ender — GDR 55:65 WR	G	G
Petra Priemer — GDR 56:49	S	S
Enith Brigitha — HOL 56:65	B	G
Kim Peyton — USA 56:81	-	S

200-METER BUTTERFLY

	1976	Review
Andrea Pollack — GDR 2:11:41 WR	G	G
Ulrike Tauber — GDR 2:12:50	S	S
Rosemarie Gabriel — GDR 2:12:86	B	B
Karen Thornton — USA 2:21:90	-	G

200-METER FREE

	1976	Review
Kornelia Ender — GDR 1:59:26 WR	G	G
Shirley Babashoff — USA 2:01:22	S	G

400-METER FREE

	1976	Review
Petra Thümer — GDR 4:09:89 WR	G	G
Shirley Babashoff — USA 4:10:46	S	G

800-METER FREE

	1976	Review
Petra Thümer — GDR 8:37:14 WR	G	G
Shirley Babashoff — USA 8:37:59	S	G
Wendy Weinberg — USA 8:42:60	B	S

100-METER BUTTERFLY

	1976	Review
Kornelia Ender — GDR 1:00:13 WR	G	G
Andrea Pollack — GDR 1:00:98	S	S
Wendy Boglioli — USA 1:01:17	B	G

4 X 100-MEDLEY RELAY

	1976	Review
GDR — Ulrike Richter, Hannelore Anke, Andrea Pollack, Kornelia Ender — 4:07:95 WR	G	G
USA — Linda Jezek, Lauri Siering, Camille Wright, Shirley Babashoff — 4:14:55	S	G

1976 Olympic results

Possible results after review

G = GOLD MEDAL
S = SILVER MEDAL
B = BRONZE MEDAL
WR = WORLD RECORD

passed her drug test), winning the silver in 8:37:59. Wendy Weinberg, also a U.S. swimmer, took the bronze in 8:42:60. In the 100-meter butterfly race, Kornelia Ender took gold and another world record in 1:00:13, while her teammate Andrea Pollack took silver in 1:00:98 and Wendy Boglioli of the United States took bronze in 1:01:17. In the 200-meter butterfly, Andrea Pollack, Ulrike Tauber, and Rosemarie Gabriel, all GDR stars with some Oral-Turinabol in their system, swept the gold, silver, and bronze medals. Finally, to put the icing on the cake, the foursome of Richter, Anke, Pollack, and Ender took gold and another world record in the 4 × 100 medley relay with a smashing time of 4:07:95, while the U.S. team of Jezek, Siering, Wright, and Babashoff took the silver in 4:14:55. The significance of this race is denoted by a greater than seven-second differential between the American team and the performance-enhanced GDR stars.

In their discussions of this issue over the past few years, Franke and Young had agreed to support each other in the quest for fairness. Knowing that the Swiss courts were not particularly friendly to outsiders (especially Americans), they had decided on an informal petition to the IOC, as opposed to straight litigation, as their first step.

Franke had also come to the United States for another reason. As a respected molecular biologist and a member of the Academy of Scientists, he felt he had a moral imperative. "I really believe that we got into the doping fight not so much for the improvement of athletics, but more importantly for the cleansing of the medical community," he said philosophically. "Sport is the just the object, but it is the collective guilt of the medical community, the scientific community, and their exploitation of human life that is so distressing," he explained with his customary intensity. "I

Winter Olympic Games, East vs. West German Medal Count

	1956 CORTINA D'AMPEZZO	1960 SQUAW VALLEY	1964 INNSBRUCK	1968 GRENOBLE	1972 SAPPORO	1976 INNSBRUCK	1980 LAKE PLACID	1984 SARAJEVO	1988 CALGARY
EAST GERMANY	1	3	4	5	14	19	23	24	25
WEST GERMANY	1	5	4	7	5	10	5	4	8

BLUE PILLS AND A LOT OF GOLD

Summer Olympic Games, East vs. West German Medal Count

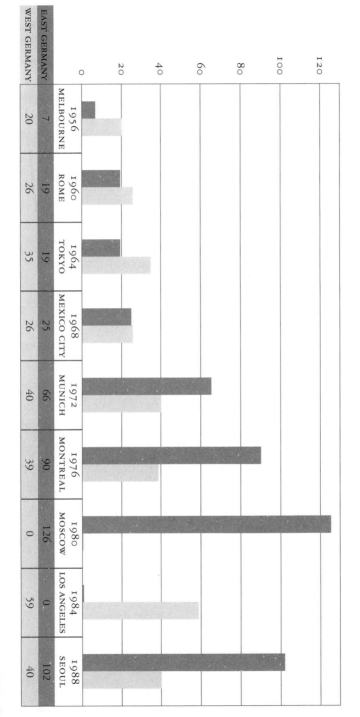

	1956 MELBOURNE	1960 ROME	1964 TOKYO	1968 MEXICO CITY	1972 MUNICH	1976 MONTREAL	1980 MOSCOW	1984 LOS ANGELES	1988 SEOUL
EAST GERMANY	7	19	19	25	66	90	126	0	102
WEST GERMANY	20	26	35	26	40	39	0	59	40

have been furious with my colleagues in the medical community for twenty-five years. We all knew that the doping experiments were going on, but nobody stood up and tried to stop it." He was sounding increasingly emphatic. "I have spoken out about the blood scandal in France with contaminated blood and the AIDS epidemic that followed. You Americans have skeletons with the Tuskegee syphilis experiments on black victims in the South. We all have collective guilt as scientists," he argued. "And then with the Third Reich and the Holocaust, we had a medical and scientific community completely silenced by fear, and no one stepped up to the plate. Look at the consequences of that denial by our professional colleagues," he said grimly.

In his fight with the courts, Franke has been somewhat of a maverick, assisting the federal prosecutors in Berlin to indict the GDR doping doctors. "It is a lonely battle for me and for Brigitte. We don't sleep much, and when we do, it is not very restful," he said. "We are threatened by former East Germans who see us as political pawns. We have been sued many times for libel and defamation by other scientists; yet we win our cases or they are dismissed. It is costly—the lawyers, the court fees—but the moral victories are huge . . . and that is why we stay in the fight." Franke tends to look at the big picture. "You know, the gene for individual courage is not on the same chromosome as that for scientific merit," he said. "We need to change this silence and denial behavior by our scientific community. There is so much at stake."

The work of Franke and his courageous wife, Brigitte Berendonk, is not going unnoticed. As the German doping trials wind down, perhaps not with the outcomes that were expected or hoped for, other markers have been put in place. There are new laws in Germany. Steroids are illegal, prescribing medications is now more severely scrutinized, and, in general, people feel secure about reporting crimes. "We have established a new benchmark in Germany," Franke said recently. "We have people, scientists, former athletes, and regular citizens, who now feel empowered to come forward and testify against these cowards of East Germany. We have had many moral and ethical victories," he reported.

If he seemed to have a sense of renewed confidence, it was with good reason. With the doping trials still in progress, Franke won a huge battle, getting the courts to reverse an earlier decision on the burden of proving bodily harm so that they no longer impose a physical examination upon victims, but instead rely on a new standard of proof—the fact that drugs were given and injections implemented. Moreover, in 1999, Brigitte was honored by a prominent group of educators with a medal acknowledging her courage and honesty in the fight against doping. And so there are small victories.

Occasionally, there is humor as well. Before he left the room after that mini-lecture to the Olympic Committee, Franke made one final point. He showed a slide of an exhausted athlete with a caption below, reading, "Maybe the whole doping problem will fade away if the advocates of ethics get tired!"

In March of 2000, an initiative presented by representative Friedhelm Julius Beucher was passed by the German Bundestag. The measure was a victims' compensation bill to assist athletes and their families who had suffered at the hands of the GDR doctors. The Organization for Doping Victims was formed under the aegis of Dr. Klaus Zöllig, with offices in Weinheim, Germany. After learning of its establishment, Franke and Berendonk took a much-needed rest.

23

Epilogue

On July 11, 2000, prosecutors in the trial of Manfred Ewald and Dr. Höppner moved toward closing arguments, first hearing from additional witnesses and then stating their intent. The prosecution called for sentences of two years in prison for each defendant—with a request for a suspended sentence for Ewald—as well as fines of 4,500 deutsche marks ($2,300 U.S. dollars).

Athletes who served as coplaintiffs, represented by Michael Lehner, wanted a stiffer sentence, pleading for a three-year prison sentence for Ewald, and a lesser one of two and a half years in jail for Dr. Höppner.

In an eleventh-hour attempt to reposition their clients before the court, the defense argued with Lehner over legal procedures. On the basis of their claim that some of the athletes did not describe the "correct color and dosage of the steroid pills," the defense pressed for additional leniency for the defendants. After apologizing for letting this legal maneuver get out of hand, Judge Dickhaus swiftly proceeded to allow Lehner to file a new motion.

It seemed that as the trial had been nearing its finish, a number of doctors who had worked under Höppner had expressed their willingness to testify for the prosecution. In a formal affidavit, Michael Lehner moved that additional physicians from Höppner's staff should be allowed to come before the court in order to clarify the dosage and administration of Oral-Turinabol. Looking squarely at Ewald, who sat passively at the defense table, he said, "Dr. Schramm told me that swimmers were given pills by the shovel. Drs. Riedel, Sünder, Koegler, Staender, should be called to testify so that we can get it straight on the record. There appears to be a huge information gap between the perpetrators and the victims. We need to hear more from the experts so that we can close this gap."

With the permission of the judge, Ines Giepel gave a closing statement on behalf of her fellow athletes. "Prosecutor Debes," she said, "pointed out the immense grief that was caused by the doping offenses. But he said grief and suffering is no element of a crime. But suffering is a psychic phenomenon, and it's one of the objectives of this trial . . . to prove that. We have proven that, we have testified about our psychological destruction, the experts have testified about the emotional and physiological damage caused by the system of coercion and force which was the result of Ewald and Höppner.

"A ruling must be measured by its ability to reflect the total destiny of harm to the individuals. I had expected to hear from Ewald and Höppner that they had done something wrong—at least an apology—but no such thing happened. A trembling voice must not be considered a mitigating factor; my voice is trembling as well. Such an attitude would be cynical."

After maintaining complete silence throughout the four-month trial, Ewald finally spoke. "My decisions do not relate at all to the things of which I have been charged," he said. "I was an elected official and I had more than a thousand friends in the GDR who cooperated with our doping program."

In their final remarks, the defense team also pointed out that "doping was not even illegal in the former East Germany." Therefore, they maintained, "although there was plenty of evidence to prove Ewald directed the GDR doping operation for twenty-five years, the judge must play by the rules and acquit him of the charge of causing bodily harm." His lawyer also reiterated that Ewald was a very sick man. Mitigating factors, he said, should include the fact that his client did arrive on time each day at the courthouse.

The verdict came on July 18, at 2 P.M. Berlin time. Manfred Ewald, "the driving force" behind the GDR doping program, was sentenced to twenty-two months in jail with probation. He was found guilty of "being an accessory to intentional bodily harm of athletes, including minors," and required to pay all court costs of the plaintiffs and the attorney's fees. His second-in-command, Dr. Höppner, was found guilty of the same charge and was sentenced to eighteen months' probation. He, too, was required to pay all fees in connection with the lengthy trial. Although prosecutors sought stiffer penalties, they agreed not to appeal. Defense attorneys said they might consider an appeal. Prosecutors noted that additional indictments against other doctors would be forthcoming on charges of inflicting more serious bodily harm.

Judge Dickhaus then asked both defendants for final statements:

EWALD: "I have nothing to add, I stand by what I did, and I am grateful."
HÖPPNER: "I would like to assure the ladies that it was not my intention to cause them deliberate physical harm. I should like to apologize for the suffering caused to some of you."

Judge Dickhaus then addressed the court:

DICKHAUS: "From the beginning of the trial there has been much media attention; many claimed that an arrangement had been made and that the trial would only last one day. A journalist wrote that it would take only one day to finish the business of the court. During the proceedings we provided all parties an opportunity to say what they had to say; you cannot please everybody, that is not our task—our task is to administer justice. This trial was not meant to judge injustice done in the GDR, it was not a political trial but a criminal proceeding. Ewald and Höppner were the driving force behind GDR doping; it is hard to imagine the tough leader as we look at this frail old man here, but this is who you were; it is hard to look behind what we see. He may have felt guilty at one time, but this did not prevent him from continuing with doping of athletes. Both defendants knew the risks of using these substances and they both accepted the dangerous side effects. The sole administration of Oral-Turinabol is a physical injury which constitutes a crime. The ends did not justify the means; the means actually did harm in the end."

Michael Lehner turned to a colleague and noted: "We are glad that they were sentenced; the damages done are not adequately reflected in the sentence. But we can live with it."

At the close of the session, athletes from all over Germany surrounded Werner Franke and Michael Lehner. In a brief ceremony on the steps of the old courthouse, they expressed their gratitude and offered flowers as a token of their appreciation.

From these athletes—some of whom had testified and others who had just supported their colleagues—Professor Franke received a smooth leather attaché case, signed by each of them. A dedication was inscribed within, reading, "Without the commitment and dedication of Werner Franke, there would never have been a doping trial."

Brigitte Berendonk did not attend the closing sessions. She was back home in Heidelberg, teaching her classes at the local school.

The story of the doping trials is actually part of a larger one—and it points to an expanding problem. As the trials wind down, there have been other developments in the world of sport as related to synthetic hormones. The steroids issue is hardly a dead one, especially in light of the recent resignation of Dr. Wade Exum, chief medical officer of the United States Olympic Committee, in protest over the reported inconsistences of drug-testing protocols in the U.S. athletic community.

There has been other fallout from the GDR doping program, as well. Recently, I was contacted by Dr. Harry Gordon (a pseudonym to protect confidentiality), a senior toxicologist and pharmacological expert at the U.S. Justice Department's Drug Enforcement Administration. For months, Gordon had been calling and faxing me requests to see some of the German archives on the doping trials. Specifically, he was looking for a connection between former GDR sports doctors and the sale of synthetic hormones in the United States.

Dr. Gordon was trying to find out how a particular drug had gotten to be so ubiquitous in the United States. "We think the former GDR docs are now exporting their science to our teenagers in the United States," he suggested over the phone. "I'm deeply concerned that now that Germany is shutting down its pervasive doping program, the scientists are looking for new markets over here." In fact, the DEA had found out belatedly that two German scientists had managed to obtain several patents for a nasal spray application for administering the drug androstenedione.

Androstenedione had been banned by the Olympic Committee, the NFL, the NBA, and the NCAA, but was still a legal and accepted supplement in major-league baseball. Mark McGwire had openly admitted to using it the year he broke Babe Ruth's and Roger Maris's hitting records, beating out the great Sammy Sosa by a small margin. Many kids, aiming to imitate McGwire's results, were now buying huge quantities of the food supplement known as Andro in health food stores.

The DEA had not put Andro on the controlled substance list and did not have the authority to do so until proper testing and outcome research had been conducted. Meanwhile, a 500-million-dollar industry was blossoming around the country and on the Internet, enabling young athletes to obtain this drug easily. Once officials at the DEA realized what was happening, they reacted with outrage.

The DEA was slow in getting involved because, under Patent Office rules, applicants for patents are not required to disclose the full history of how a drug was developed, or every possible use of the drug. In this case, apparently Rüdiger Häcker (see appendices), a scientist of the GDR doping program, had been granted a patent in the United States for a nasal spray application of androstenedione with a supporting article the basis of which was that the drug could be used to treat Parkinson's disease. However, the DEA had reason to suspect that the application did not include the supporting documentation most relevant to the drug's use, which by the dates of publication and subject indicated that the spray would have been developed under the auspices of the GDR doping program.

In a letter to Werner Franke, Gordon expressed the paradox raised by the history of this patent: "How is it that Rüdiger Häcker," he wrote, "a central figure in the former East German government doping program, can capitalize (i.e., be granted patents) on information gathered from the program when other scientists have been or will be tried in German court for their participation in the program?"

The question of whether the DEA can stem the flow of unwanted information (not to mention unethical commercial gain) in this area will have to be answered elsewhere. But this episode indicates a need not only for close monitoring of drug sales and patent applications, but for questioning the ease with which drugs in general are taken or administered.

Meanwhile, while it remains the ultimate arena for inter-national sporting competition, the Olympics, no longer assumed to be a stronghold of fairness, are the object of increasing scrutiny—relative to drugs and influence.

The financial stakes involving the Olympics increased enormously in the late 1980s. Shortly after the meetings with Ewald in Berlin in 1985, Samaranch and members of his inner IOC circle began to unveil TOP, better known as The Olympic Program, a series of sponsorship opportuni-ties for wealthy corporate executives and their families, bringing in unprecedented revenues of $100 million on the eve of the 1988 Seoul Olympics. Nine companies signed on for the Olympic roller-coaster ride; Coca-Cola, Visa, Brother, FedEx, 3M, Time-Life, Panasonic, Kodak, and Phillips joined the 100-million-dollar club of corporate sponsors . . . all for the rights to see those five rings under their name and logo.

In 1992, NBC got in on the action by paying $400 mil-lion for the rights to televise the Barcelona Olympics. In 1994, the IOC saw more dollar signs when they shifted to a two-year cycle of winter and summer Olympics on even years instead of the traditional quadrennium. The potential for more cash was unlimited. The NBC contract quickly jumped to $1 billion in 1994 alone. All of the major spon-sorships were faced with a serious dose of reality when in 1988, the superstar hero of the Seoul Olympics, Ben John-son, tested positive for stanazolol, a steroid, and was stripped of his gold medal, in a drama that played out in billions of households, carried live on television to over 200 countries. All of a sudden, the rings of the Olympic movement did not have the same magic.

In late 1999, Senator John McCain of Arizona called for hearings on another Olympic scandal. It was the peddling of Olympic sites for cash, scholarships, and world-class shopping sprees. His Senate hearings in Washington forced Olympic officials, including chief counsel François Carrard and IOC boss Samaranch, to swear in and be held accountable for alleged bribery and unlawful conduct. Senator McCain and former senator George Mitchell have pressed for a housecleaning of IOC corruption. Eleven members of the IOC board resigned over allegations of wrongdoing. More are expected to step down as the Salt Lake City Winter Games begin.

APPENDICES

APPENDIX I

Abbreviated Chronology of
Doping, including GDR Program,
as of July 1, 2000

- In 1904, Tom Hanks won the marathon in the St. Louis Olympics and subsequently lapsed into a coma. He had ingested brandy and strychnine before the race.

- In 1952, a cyclist died during the Helsinki Olympics after using amphetamines and coffee.

- In 1957, the American Medical Association appointed a special commission to look at the abuse of amphetamines in elite athletics.

- In 1958, a survey conducted by the American College of Sports Medicine found that more than 35 percent of a sample of 441 coaches recommended the amphetamine Benzedrine.

- In 1958 Brigitte Berendonk, a seventeen-year-old elite athlete, defected to West Germany with her parents and siblings.

- In 1960, at the Rome Olympics, a Danish cyclist died of a mixture of amphetamines and alcohol and a sprint athlete died of a heroin overdose.

- In 1962, the IOC passed the first resolution against "doping."

- In 1965, VEB Jenapharm, a German pharmaceutical company, synthesized the anabolic steroid Oral-Turinabol, which allowed enhancement of athletes' testosterone levels.

- In 1967, a letter was written accompanied by a chapter from a well-known medical text (edited by Drs. Hauschild and Görisch) that outlined the dangerous side effects of Oral-Turinabol, a drug created by Jenapharm.

- In 1967, the IOC established a medical commission to control drug use.

- In 1968, after announcing the first drug-testing program at the Mexico City Olympics, Colonel F. Don Miller of the USOC noted, "We must obliterate the image of the chemical athlete."

- On September 29, 1970, Dr. Manfred Höppner, director of sports medicine for all of East Germany, authorized the use of performance-enhancement drugs (including steroids) to prepare for the upcoming 1972 Olympics. (Source is *Süddeutsche Zeitung* newspaper.)

- In 1970, a survey of ninety-three professional athletes on thirteen NFL teams revealed that 61 percent used amphetamines.

- On September 10, 1972, at the Munich Olympics, Brigitte Berendonk, competing for West Germany, noticed that her competitors (Hartmut Briesnick, Dieter Hoffmann, Rothenburg, Thorith, and Sachse) were clearly doped.

- In 1972, at the Munich Olympics, American swimmer Rick DeMont was disqualified and lost his gold medal for using a prescription drug indicated for asthma.

- In 1972, just after Munich, the first official record of forty-two top Olympic athletes who were doped was found. The documents record the throwing history of Margitta Gummel, gold medalist in 1968 and the first GDR athlete ever to be doped.

- In 1973, George Sievers, age sixteen, a GDR athlete, collapsed and died at poolside while training. His parents were not allowed to see the autopsy report. However, today, new documents show that his cause of death was most likely attributed to a ruptured heart from anabolic steroid overloads.

- In 1974, a nine-page document called the Central Committee Report was created outlining the first GDR doping experiments on elite athletes.

- In 1976, prior to the Montreal Games, seven U.S. swimmers tested positive for banned substances. At the Games a few months later, 2.9 percent of those tested were positive, including two athletes who won gold medals and one who was a silver medalist.

- A 1976 track and field federation report stated that there were thirty-five cases of steroid use in ten different countries, but *not a single positive case* from Germany.

- In 1976, a special conference was held in the Black Forest of Germany, where sport doctors Klümper, Mader, and Hollmann declared that doping was not a medical problem but a question of ethics.

- In 1976, Dr. Mader came to West Germany to promote the use of steroids. He was a major proponent of injecting teenage women with anabolics.

- In 1976, just prior to the Montreal Olympic Games, Berendonk confronted Dr. Mader about injecting female athletes and asked him to stop.

- In 1976, after the Montreal Olympics, a group of scientists from the University of Leipzig were honored for their "excellent results in doping results" and given a prize of 100,000 DM for science and technology.

- At the 1976 Games, East German swimmers won eleven out of thirteen swim events.

- On February 26, 1977, Berendonk, the whistle-blower, published all evidence of doping in the *Süddeutsche Zeitung*.

- In 1977 (September 28, 1977) doping expert and lawyer Dr. Wolfgang Schäuble declared at a conference that "doping should be used in a limited way and under control of doctors' supervision so that athletes can still compete in the arena of sport."

- In 1980, swimmer Kristin Otto won the first of her six gold medals. (She is now a TV commentator for German ZDF.)

- In 1980, Rica Reinisch won three gold medals in the Moscow Olympics and then quit the sport two years later. She was later diagnosed with ovarian cysts due to the high level of testosterone in her system.

- In 1981, pharmaceutical company Zimet and Kombinat Germed formulated a plan to mask illegal drugs by using "bridge therapy" so that steroids would not be detected during urine testing.

- In 1981, scientist Michael Öttel participated in a symposium that offered information that would circumvent IOC drug testing.

- In 1982, Catherine Menschner had to retire early from swimming because of complications from steroid injections. Meunschner was fourteen when she was paralyzed by an overload of testosterone.

- In 1982, Birgit Heukrodt became a three-time world champion in freestyle swimming under trainer Rolf Gläser. (He was convicted of doping charges in the summer of 1998.)

- In 1983, at the Pan American Games, seventeen athletes, including two from the United States, were disqualified for using anabolic steroids. Eleven U.S. athletes decided not to submit to testing and withdrew from competition.

- Beginning on January 12, 1984, Dr. Helmut Riedel kept a handwritten workbook describing the drugs, dosage levels, timetables, and names for some two hundred track and field athletes.

- In 1984, after the Los Angeles Olympics, eight U.S. cyclists admitted that they had "blood doped," or stored their blood and reinfused it prior to competition.

- In 1984, the publication of *Death in the Locker Room* (Goldman, 1984) reported eleven deaths and fourteen cases of liver cancer among athletes using steroids.

- In early 1985, GDR chief Manfred Ewald wrote and published a book entitled *I Was Sport,* admitting widespread use of performance-enhancement drugs and acknowledging their benefits to the improvement of sport.

- In 1985, an NCAA survey of 2,000 college athletes from eleven schools revealed that 27 percent of respondents used marijuana, 12 percent used cocaine, 11 percent used major painkillers, and 82 percent used alcohol frequently.

- In 1986, Professor Öhme, of the Academy of Sciences, made "substance P" a code name for neuropeptides available to fencers and gymnasts. Neuropeptides were especially useful in dealing with stress and emotional problems in certain types of risk-taking events.

- In 1986, a letter was written by Olympian Marita Koch to Dr. Michael Öttel, the director of research at VEB Jenapharm, complaining that "my drugs were not as potent as the ones that were given to my opponent Barbel Eckert, who kept beating me." This was known as "dope-envy" in the GDR.

- In 1987, the GDR sports leaders changed the code for their STS 646 state plan for doping so that they would not be detected. Common doping drugs like Oral-Turinabol were now called "M1"; the drug mestanolone was now called "M2."

- In March 1988, an experimental drug known as androstenedione, which is the precursor to testosterone, was introduced as a nasal spray. (This was the same drug that Mark McGwire would later use.) It did not prove successful, and actually destroyed German swimmer Raik Hannemann's nasal system.

- In 1988, a secret report known as the Staatsplanthema 14.25, or state doping plan, was found.

- In 1988 at the Seoul Games, in addition to Ben Johnson, eight other athletes tested positive and were disqualified. Both the Hungarian and Bulgarian weight-lifting teams withdrew from competition and went home.

- In 1988, Anavar, the steroid made by the drug company Searle, was taken off the market because of illegal use.

- In 1989, the GDR conducted experiments with sixteen to eighteen-year-old athletes by giving them high daily dosages of 20 mg Oral-Turinabol and mestanolone to test their performance effects.

- In 1989, a scientist at the University of Dresden introduced a new drug called Piracetam, which was to enhance aggression and control it for certain types of events.

- In 1989, a prominent sports doctor, Hans-Georg Aschenbach, gave a detailed press conference to the magazine *Bild* about GDR doping practices.

- In 1989, in testimony before the Senate Judiciary Committee led by Senator Joe Biden, American sprinter Diane Williams testified that she first received Anavar and then later Dianabol from her coach. The drug made her run faster, but she stopped menstruating and grew hair on her face. She noted at the hearing: "I behaved like a nymphomaniac, I had no control over my sexuality, and my clitoris grew to an embarrassing size."

- In October 1989, the executive board of the USOC approved the most comprehensive random drug-testing program ever implemented. The program included an outside auditor and coordinated the forty-one national governing bodies of individual sports.

- In the fall of 1989, the USOC and the Soviet Union agreed to a mutual testing program, including a worldwide computer system to monitor athletes' test results.

- In 1989, a document was found that identified doping researchers Professor Winfred Schaeker, Dr. Kluemper, and Dr. Helmut Riedel, all members of the Institute for Sport at the University of Leipzig.

- In 1989, a known doping doctor, Dr. Helmut Riedel, wrote a dissertation thesis entitled: *A report about steroids and their effects on development in track and field* and sold parts of his research to the German magazine *Stern*.

- In 1990, the first GDR athlete to come forward and disclose widespread doping was gold-medal swimmer Christiane Knacke-Sommer, who told the magazine *Stern* that she was full of anabolics.

- In 1990, the Dubin Commission was convened by Judge Dubin of Canada to investigate doping practices among Canadian athletes, including gold-medal sprinter Ben Johnson.

- In 1990, the magazine *Der Spiegel* published an extensive confession of coach Michael Regner, of how he doped his swimmers in the GDR before he moved to New Zealand to start a new life.

- In March of 1990, German scholars started publishing their work in academic journals on the use of anabolic steroids in sport, especially Professor Klingberg of Karl Marx University in Leipzig.

- In April of 1990, Dr. Manfred Höppner, a prominent sports official in the GDR, ordered that all documents relating to sport and doping be shredded.

- In December of 1990, Berendonk and Franke made a special trip to the military hospital at Bad Saarow and located one copy of the secret files called Dissertation B.

- In September 1991, Dr. Dietrich Hannemann, director of sports medicine for the former GDR, said at a world conference on antidoping that it was "time to safeguard the health of our athletes."

- In 1993, a liver tumor was discovered in the body of swim champion Dr. Birgit Heukrodt, today a noted Berlin surgeon.

- In early 1994, antidoping advocate and former Olympian Brigitte Berendonk went on television with Manfred Ewald, accused him of lying, and declared that someday she would take him to court.

- In 1995, Rica Reinisch, a former East German gold medalist, came forward to accuse her coach, Uwe Neumann, of systematic doping of his athletes.

- In August of 1997, Ulrike Tauber, 1975 world champion and 1976 gold medalist in Montreal, gave an interview to the newspaper *Süddeutsche Zeitung* and confessed to the ingestion of small packages of blue tabs waiting for her and others poolside at daily workouts.

- In 1997, a 177-page report prepared by sixty Berlin prosecutors, which represented the first wave of indictments against trainers, coaches, and doctors of the former GDR, was filed.

- In September of 1997, prosecutors documented 1,047 cases of systematic doping of elite GDR athletes.

- Also in September 1997, Uwe Neumann, well-known GDR trainer, was fired from the German Federation of Sport for giving steroids to minors.

- On October 7, 1997, prosecutors charged Dieter Lindemann and Volker Frischke with giving drugs to minors with "intent to do bodily harm." They ultimately paid penalties in exchange for having the charges dropped.

- On October 14, 1997, prosecutors in Berlin charged swim coaches Rolf Gläser and Dieter Krause with doping young swimmers. Gläser was later convicted, and Krause paid penalties in exchange for having the charges dropped.

- In March of 1998, the Associated Press reported that government files in Germany disclosed that 10,000 East German athletes were doped over thirty years.

- Also in March of 1998, *Der Spiegel* reported that the STASI police and Dr. Manfred Höppner ordered athletes to terminate pregnancies because of possible mutations and deformities from steroid use.

- On March 18, 1998, the first Berlin trial began. Four trainers and two doctors of SC Dynamo Swim club were indicted for "doing bodily harm to minors."

- On June 3, 1998, four-time record holder and 1977 European swim champion Carola Nitschke Beraktschjan admitted to being doped and said that she was returning her medals and asking/that the record books be expunged.

- On June 5, 1998, swimmer Christiane Knacke-Sommer, bronze medalist in the 1980 Olympics, testified about being doped and asked that her medals and records be returned.

- On June 5, 1998, Andreas Krieger (known as Heidi before a sex change) told of doping during 1986 World Championships, and returned medals.

- Just prior to testifying on June 5, 1998, Krieger and Sommer asked for police protection through their lawyers Michael Lehner and Christian Paschen. Their lives had been threatened.

- On June 15, 1998, Professor Werner Franke brought a private lawsuit against German sport officials Manfred von Richthofen, Jochen Kuehl, and Harm Beyer (of FINA) for allegedly failing to disclose and covering up details of doping and for doing injury to young athletes.

- On July 7, 1998, Dr. Dieter Binus, a fifty-nine-year-old physician, admitted in a Berlin trial to doping a large number of swimmers as chief swim physician from 1969 through 1986.

- In July of 1998, Sylvia Gerasch, a former GDR swimming Olympian (and a West German 1996 Olympian) testified in the Berlin doping trials about her use of steroids.

- In July 1998, prior to her testimony, Gerasch was granted a restraining order that prevented expert doctors for the defense from giving athletes an ob/gyn examination, data that might cause embarrassment and humiliation in the courtroom.

- In July of 1998, Steven Ungerleider traveled to Berlin to witness the trials, interview doctors, lawyers, whistle-blowers, and athlete victims.

- On August 18, 1998, a new trial began, with indictments against five trainers and doctors of the TSC Berlin Swim Club.

- On August 18, 1998, Dr. Dorit Rösler, age fifty, testified that she had doped teenagers. She was confronted in the courtroom by former swim champion Karen König, who asked her why she did it and if she would do it again.

- On August 24, 1998, the first verdict was announced; the Berlin court convicted two doctors and one trainer from the TSC Club and fined them 7,000 to 27,000 DM.

- On August 25, 1998, Deutsche Telecom, the equivalent of US WEST, gave $1 million to set up an experimental testing lab in Germany.

- On August 31, 1998, coach Rolf Gläser, fifty-eight, was fined 7,200 DM and Dr. Dieter Binus, notorious swim doctor, was fined 9,000 DM.

- On September 11, 1998, a new law went into effect in Germany that mandated a sixteen-year prison sentence for anyone prescribing or using performance-enhancement drugs.

- On October 8, 1998, three-time Boston Marathon winner and German athlete Utta Pippig was suspended for a positive drug test for testosterone.

- On October 20, 1998, German sports chief Manfred Ewald was forcibly ejected from a Berlin courtroom because the judge had determined that he would have to testify later.

- In October 1998, Ralph Reichenbach, a world-class shot-putter, died suddenly of a heart attack due to an enlarged heart caused by steroid use, as reported by the German press.

- On December 7, 1998, Dr. Bernd Pansold plea-bargained and was fined 14,400 DM. He filed an appeal and it was denied by a higher court.

- On October 22, 1999, vice president of the German Sports Federation, Horst Röder was convicted and given a one-year suspended jail sentence and fined.

- November 1, 1999, Röder wrote letters to former athletes apologizing for his harm and asking forgiveness.

- On December 22, 1999, Egon Müller, former general secretary of the Swim Federation, and two trainers were given one-year suspended jail sentences and fined 5,000 DM.

- On January 12, 2000, the GDR doctor and senior medical person for swimming, Dr. Lothar Kipke, was given a fifteen-month suspended jail sentence and ordered to pay a large fine.

- On April 28, 2000, former GDR sports chief Manfred Ewald was indicted on 142 counts of causing bodily harm to minors. Ewald was both president of the German Sports Federation and chief of the Olympic Committee from 1961 to 1988.

- On April 29, 2000, thirty-two former elite and Olympic swimmers brought civil charges against Ewald in addition to the criminal indictments. Ewald had supervised the chief doctor, Manfred Höppner.

- On April 30, 2000, Judge Walter Neuhaus suddenly became sick and had to step down from the court proceedings.

- On April 30, 2000, Judge Dirk Dickhaus, thirty-five years old, was asked to preside over the Ewald and Höppner trials. Dickhaus limited the number of media credentials, citing lack of space in the courtroom, and rejected media requests from German TV, the *Frankfurter Allgemeine, Sender Freies Berlin,* and the *New York Times*.

- On May 2, 2000, the trial of Dr. Manfred Höppner and Manfred Ewald opened in Berlin.

- On May 6, 2000, Dr. Höppner told the court that he apologized for doping, but claimed that he was not in violation of the laws of the GDR.

- On May 6, 2000, Höppner noted that the late Florence Joyner Griffith, the double gold medalist from America, was so heavily doped that he felt compelled to dope his sprinters in an attempt to beat the Americans.

- On May 10, 2000, Berlin prosecutor Klaus Heinrich Debes agreed to allow the defense to have Manfred Ewald evaluated by a psychiatrist and a physician to see if he was fit to stand trial.

- On June 5, 2000, Dr. Wade Exum, chief medical officer of the USOC, resigned and angrily denounced U.S. policy of covering up drug tests. He threatened a lawsuit the next day.

APPENDIX II

Documents

Deutsches Krebsforschungszentrum
Forschungsschwerpunkt A *Krebsentstehung und Differenzierung*

German Cancer Research Center
Research Program A *Cell Differentiation and Carcinogenesis*

Dr. Steven Ungerleider
Integrated Research Services
66 Club Road, Suite 370
Eugene, OR 97401
USA

Abteilung für Zellbiologie/A0100
Division of Cell Biology/A0100

Prof. Dr. Werner W. Franke

Im Neuenheimer Feld 280
D-69120 Heidelberg/FRG
Telefax: ++49 (0)6221 42-3404
Telephone Secretary: ++49 (0)6221 42-3400
Telephone Direct: ++49 (0)6221 42-3212

Heidelberg, 21 September 1999

Dear Steven,

please find attached four important documents, all verdicts that have been accepted directly, i.e., without a public court case, comparable to a "guilty plea" in the USA.

1) The verdict against Dr. Dietberg Freiberg, deputy and "right hand executive" of Dr. Manfred Höppner in the Sports Medical Service, for a total of 6 months prison;

2) Dr. Dietrich Hannemann, former deputy director of the Sports Medical Service (a position parallel to that of Dr. Höppner but not in the "Doping Drug Department"), for a total of DM 45.000,- (approx. US $ 25.000,-);

3) Dr. Horst Tausch, chief physician of the National Swimming Team of the GDR since 1985, for a total of 10 months prison;

4) Mr. Uwe Neumann, swimming coach of the Club "SC Einheit Dresden" - and until approx. one year ago functioning as coach in the present German Swimming Association -, for a total of DM 8.000,-.

The two sentences to imprisonment were postponed on probation with the request of other duties, including a letter of apology by Dr. Tausch to the female swimmers he had doped (see copy of letter through his lawyers to former 4×100 m free style world record holder Karen König). This letter is also a general confession.

Please note that in each of these verdicts the names of the swimmers damaged are specifically mentioned together with the specific damage: As this is sensitive information, it should not be mentioned in any publication in a way that allows to relate the damage or disease to the specific athlete.

I will ship you more verdicts and decisions in the next week.

With best regards,

Werner W. Franke

Letter of correspondence between author (Ungerleider) and Professor Werner Franke regarding the verdicts and plea bargains of Drs. Freiberg, Hannemann, Tausch, and coach Neumann, prominent figures in the GDR doping scandal.

Deutsches Krebsforschungszentrum
Forschungsschwerpunkt A Krebsentstehung und Differenzierung
German Cancer Research Center
Research Program A Cell Differentiation and Carcinogenesis

Dr. Steven Ungerleider
Integrated Research Services
66 Club Road, Suite 370
Eugene, OR 97401
USA

Abteilung für Zellbiologie/A0100
Division of Cell Biology/A0100

Prof. Dr. Werner W. Franke

Im Neuenheimer Feld 280
D-69120 Heidelberg/FRG
Telefax: ++49 (0)6221 42-3404
Telephone Secretary: ++49 (0)6221 42-3400
Telephone Direct: ++49 (0)6221 42-3212

Heidelberg, 14 October 1999

Dear Steven,

just in the moment when I had asked my secretary to send you the next pack of verdicts from the court in Berlin, I received your e-mail/fax.

The only person really involved and up-to-date with all the documents and court materials is the undersigned. I have to push and drive the prosecutors now in several states of the former GDR by specific letters, incriminating documents etc. Dr. Lehner and his colleagues are so friendly to provide the professional framework but of course nobody could pay lawyers' fees in this gigantic undertaking. So any final decision will be sent to you immediately. Herein you find the following verdicts:

1) **Dr. Dietrich Hannemann**, former Deputy Director and Head Physician of the Sports Medical Service (SMD) of the GDR, who was head of a department not directly involved in the drug system but of course also involved in the decision-making. The total fine was DM 45,000 (~ US$ 23,690);

2) **Dr. Horst Röder**, Vice President of the DTSB, the general sports organization of the GDR, who received a verdict of one year prison (if a person is sentenced for the first time and less than two years of prison, it will be on probation);

3) **Dr. Thomas Köhler**, the other Vice President of the DTSB, specific for winter sports, for a total fine of DM 26,400 (~ US$ 13,900);

4) **Dr. Hans-Günther Rabe**, the Head Coach of the entire GDR team, who was not directly involved in the personal drug treatment but in the upper decision-making, for a total of seven months of prison;

5) **Dr. Elke Schramm**, one of the assistants of Dr. Manfred Höppner, for a total of six months of prison;

6) **Dr. Hans-Jürgen Schmidt**, also an assistant of Dr. Höppner, for a total fine of DM 12,600 (~ US$ 6,600).

Letter of correspondence between author (Ungerleider) and Professor Werner Franke regarding the guilty verdicts of Drs. Hannemann, Röder, Kohler, Rabe, Schramm, and Schmidt, prominent figures in the GDR doping scandal.

Landgericht Berlin

Der Vorsitzende der Strafkammer 34

10559 Berlin, Turmstraße 91
Fernruf (Vermittlung): 90 14 - 0, Intern: (914)
Apparatnummer: siehe (☎)
Telefax: (030) 90 14 - 2010
PostbankKto der Justizkasse Berlin:
Bln 3 52-108 (BLZ 100 100 10)

Fahrverbindung:
U-Bhf. Turmstraße, S-Bhf. Bellevue
Bus 123, 167, 227, 245

Landgericht Berlin, Postanschrift: 10548 Berlin

Herrn
Dr. Steven Ungerleider
Psychologe
Integrated Research Inc.
66 Clud Road
Eugene, Oregon 97401

Geschäftszeichen	Ihr Zeichen	Bearbeiter	☎	Datum

Sehr geehrter Herr Dr. Ungerleider!

Anliegend übersende ich Ihnen das Urteil der Strafkammer 34 des Landgerichts Berlin gegen Dr. Pansold und den Beschluss des Bundesgerichtshofes, in dem dieser das Urteil bestätigt hat.

Mit freundlichen Grüßen

Bräutigam
Vorsitzender Richter am Landgericht

Letter of correspondence and thank-you note from federal Judge Hansgeorg Bräutigam to the author (Ungerleider) after his interview.

Staatsanwaltschaft II
bei dem Landgericht Berlin

10559 Berlin, den 30.07.1999
Alt-Moabit 100
Tel.-Nr.: 9014-6930

28 Js 14/98

An das
Landgericht Berlin
- Große Strafkammer -

A n k l a g e s c h r i f t

1. Manfred **Ewald**,

   geboren am 17. Mai 1926 in Podejuch,

   wohnhaft: Berliner Str. 6f, 14797 Damsdorf,

   Deutscher,

   – Registerauszug ist beigefügt –

   Verteidiger:

   Rechtsanwältin Brigitte Sonntag,

   Büschingstr. 1, 10249 Berlin

2. Dr. Manfred **Höppner**,

   geboren am 16. April 1934 in Weinböhla/Meißen,

   wohnhaft: Karl-Marx-Allee 84, 10243 Berlin,

   Deutscher,

   – Registerauszug ist beigefügt –

   Verteidiger:

   Rechtsanwalt Hans-Peter Mildebrath,

   Brandenburgische Str. 43, 10707 Berlin

Announcement of the formal criminal indictments against doping chief
Manfred Ewald and his deputy, Dr. Manfred Höppner.

Case Number: **522 - 40/99**

With Regard to the Criminal Case

against   1.   Egon M ü l l e r
              born December 20, 1926 in Leipzig
              residing at: Haushoferstraße 13 a, 12487 Berlin
              German National

          Defense: Osterloh, Attorney at Law

          2.   Dr. Lothar K i p k e
               born January 1, 1928 in Breslau
               residing at: Nachtigallenweg 13
                            Waldsteinberg
               German National

          Defense: Dr. E. J. Schöppe, Attorney at Law

          3.   Wolfgang R i c h t e r
               born March 19, 1937 in Dresden
               residing in Gava/Barcelona, Calle Tamarit,
               House No. 7-8, Spain
               German National

          Defense: Gunther B., Grübler, Attorney at Law

          4.   Jürgen Dieter T a n n e b e r g e r,
               born October 30, 1943 in Plauen
               residing at Kolhagenstaße 30, 40593 Düsseldorf
               German National   .

          Defense: Dr. Dieter Bolz, Attorney at Law

Charge: Bodily Injury

Announcement of the formal verdicts in the criminal trials against Egon
Müller, Dr. Lothar Kipke, Wolfgang Richter, and Jürgen Tanneberger.

Pressekarte Nr. Ⅰ *13.07.98*

(Nur in Verbindung mit dem Personal- und Presseausweis gültig)

für den Prozeß gegen *Gläser, Rolf u.a.*

vor dem *LG*

Name: *Ungerleider, Steven*

Zeitung: *Integrated*

Bei Verlust kein Ersatz!

■ [SENJ 6]

Press credential provided to author (Ungerleider) by the Federal court officials in Berlin for the July 1998 trial of Rolf Gläser.

U.S. Department of Justice

Drug Enforcement Administration

Washington, D.C. 20537

November 13, 1998

Prof. Dr. Werner W. Franke
Deutsches Krebsforschungszentrum
Abteilung für Zellbiologie/A0100
Im Neuenheimer Feld 280
D-69120 Heidelberg/FRG

Dear Prof. Dr. Franke:

I received your fax dated October 26th. I thank you for the information provided. Over the last week, I have gathered some additional documents and information that may be of interest to you. I am now going to fax these additional documents to you. Due to some of the problems with the fax machine here at DEA Headquarters, it may be necessary to fax this material to you separately, rather than in one lump sum.

The first two documents are additional United States patents. The first is United States Patent 5,756,071 granted May 26, 1998 and entitled "Method for Nasally Administering Aerosols of Therapeutic Agents to Enhance Penetration of the Blood Brain Barrier." The inventors are Claudia Mattern and Rudiger Hacker. Among other things, this patent describes the nasal administration of testosterone and the lowering of the testosterone/epitestosterone ratio. The second document is United States Patent 5,591,732 granted January 7, 1997 and entitled "Medicament for Influencing the Degree of Activation of the Central Nervous System." Claudia Mattern and Rudiger Hacker were also the inventors of this patent. This patent, among other things, discusses the anabolic effects of Oral Turinabol and mestanolone.

There are several points of interest regarding the two patents mentioned above as well as United States Patent 5,578,588 which I faxed to you on October 23rd, 1998. One is the earliest dates mentioned under the category of "Foreign Application Priority Data". They are either May or June of 1992. This suggest that the data to support all three of these patents were available at least by May and June 1992. The second point is the failure to identity any scientific or medical journal articles written by Mattern and Hacker in which is provided the data supporting these patents (at least from the standpoint of anabolic steroids). I have had the DEA library do an extensive search of past publications of which Hacker and/or Mattern were authors. In the 1980s Hacker did, in fact, author a number of papers that appeared primarily in the journals, Medizin and Sport and Theorie und Praxis Leistungssport. Claudia Mattern was not a coauthor on any of these papers. Based just on a reading of the titles of these references, there is no indication to me that any of these articles pertained to data that would subsequently be used to

Letter of correspondence from the United States Department of Justice, Drug Enforcement Agency (DEA), to expert Professor Werner Franke regarding a very sensitive subject matter.

support any of the three patents mentioned above. There were identified a number of articles authored by Hacker and Mattern, as well as others, that appeared between 1993 and 1998. None of the articles pertained to anabolic steroids. Several articles did pertain to the intranasal administration of drugs to treat Parkinson's disease. This topic was mentioned in United States Patent 5,756,071. One interesting reference revealed in the literature search is what appears to be a book on sports doping written by Rudiger Hacker and published in 1991. The DEA library has already identified a source for this book and has made a request to borrow the book via interlibrary loan.

I can think of several possibilities as to why I have not been able to identify scientific literature pertaining to the steroid portions of the three documents mentioned. One possibility is that the computer searches conducted by the DEA library just did not pick up the additional articles. This seems unlikely considering that DEA subscribes to a number of computerized scientific databases, all of which were checked. A second possibility is that Hacker and Mattern simply elected not to publish the data even though they had patent protection dating back to June 1992. This also seems unlikely considering the pressures placed on scientists (certainly in the U.S. but I would also assume in other countries e.g. Germany) to publish. A third possibility is that the data in these patents may have been generated all or in part through the former East German doping program. For a variety of reasons that I shall not go into, I would think that it would be difficult to get such data published in scientific and medical journals. At least in the United States there would be much less of a problem to use the data to obtain a patent. The degree of scientific scrutiny applied to publish an article in most scientific journals is greater than the scientific scrutiny applied to approving a patent application.

I am also faxing to you the copy of a document that I believe contains the specific information used by the U.S. Patent examiner in approving United States Patent 5,578,588 dealing with nasal spray application of androstenedione. In spending time over at the patent office, I have learned that for each approved patent there is a public file which is supposed to contain all the information used by the patent examiner in making a decision to approve the patent. Also included is all the correspondence between the inventors and the patent office. Late last week, I made arrangements to review the public file for United States Patent 5,578,588. In that file I found a document sent from Rudiger Hacker to the Assistant Commissioner for Patents. The document was actually sent via the patent law firm of Merchant, Gould, Smith, Edell, Welter and Schmidt. In that document was found information on the experimental protocol used and on the data collected, including several graphs. An identical document was also sent by Claudia Mattern. A question of particular interest to me is whether or not the experimental protocol and the data obtained to support U.S. Patent 5,578,588 was, in fact, generated as part of the East German doping program. It may be possible to answer this question by comparing the information in this document with all the information that you and your wife have uncovered concerning the East German doping program.

The same question just asked can also be applied to United States Patents 5,756,071 and 5,591,732. In other words, was the data used to approve these patents actually generated as part of the East German government doping program of the 1970s and 1980s? If the answer is yes for any of these patents, then in my mind a certain paradox is raised. This paradox can be expressed

Continuation of DEA letter to Professor Franke.

in the following question: How is it that Rudiger Hacker, a central figure in the former East German government doping program, can capitalize (e.g. be granted patents) on information gathered from the program when other scientist have been or will be tried in a German court for their participation in the program? This question probably best simply illustrates my ignorance concerning this topic matter.

Please note that I have now had several conversations with Dr. Steven Ungerleider. I have promised to fax him the same documents that I have given to you. I have asked him for any information that he may have on the East German experimentation with androstenedione. I will also be asking him whether or not the protocol and data found in the document I obtained from the patent file for U.S. Patent 5,578,588 (German Patent Equivalent DE 4214953 C2) is similar or identical to that found in the East German doping documents that his group is now translating. Simply put, I am now interested in knowing as much as possible about the background behind this patent which is mentioned in numerous advertisements and in newspaper and magazine articles dealing with androstenedione.

Finally, let me briefly discuss the request that you made of me in your fax of October 26th. A search under the heading of "androstenedione" using just about any of the Internet search engines will provide Internet web sites that either advertize or discuss androstenedione. I have found a considerable number of such web sites by using the metacrawler search engine (www.metacrawler.com). From what I have been told, this particular search engine actually searches across other search engines such as Yahoo.

I would appreciate any information that you or Dr. Ungerleider can provide concerning experimentation with androstenedione during the East German doping program. I also look forward to the publication of your wife's book in the English language. This is a topic area that has been and continues to be of interest to me.

Sincerely,

Continuation of DEA letter to Professor Franke.

Name	Club	T-0	T-0
Krause, Barbara	Dyn.		1 600
Pollak	"		1 600 "
Knacke	"		1 600 "
Lang	"		200 "
Witt	"		200 "
Diers	K.M.St.	1230 ~~370~~	~~200~~
Mahne	"	1355 ~~225~~	200
Zipke	"	1230 ~~430~~	200
Schneider	"	1355 ~~1095~~	200
Täuber	"	1355 ~~1095~~	200
Greuenister	"	1230 ~~370~~	200
Waldke	E. Werd.	970	—
Löbel	"	1355	200
Reinisch	"	1230	200
Treiber	"	1355	200
Geier	"	545	200
Metschuck	SC Emp-Rost	1355	200
Linke	"	970	—
Oeilk	"	970	—
Hille	SC Mgdl.	555	—
Hille	"	985	—
Riedel	"	945	200
Schmidt	SC H Hall	1250	200
Schäurich	"	1205	200

STASI secret police files of GDR athletes, their respective clubs, and the dosages of drugs to be administered to them for training and competition.

46

Männer :

Vom 3.1. – 30.1.77
27.2. – 6.3.77
25.4. – 22.5.77
6.6. – 3.7.77

zwischen 200 u. 400 mgr.
Turinabol – zwischen –
durch bekommen sie
Testostropin (männl.
formon)

70 Kader für Länderkampf mit der Sowjetunion

Vom 25.2. – 4.4.77
25.5. – 5.7.77

Vitamin B 17 (bis 8 Tabletten)
am Tag
dieses B 17 wird im Labor des
Arzneimittelwerkes Dresden ausschließlich für das FKS herges.
zusätzlich werden 4 x 2 Tabl.
Dioktazit (Ferment zur
Aktivierung des Stoffwechsels,
verabreicht

Folgende Die Nationalmannschaftskader erhalten in der Zeit vom 1.7. – 5.7.77 bis zu
5 Infusionen Glukose, die durch die Sektionsärzte im VD-Buch nachweispflichtig sind.

Folgende Sektionsärzte sind einbezogen :

SC Empor Rostock	Dr. Ingendorf	SHB
SC Dynamo Bln.	Binius Dieter	SHB Dyn.
TSC Berlin	Dr. Schneider (Männer)	SHB
	Dr. Fehling Ute (Frauen)	"
SC Magdeburg	Kegel	SHB
ASK Potsdam (Rostock)	Dr. Kamke Wolfg.	SHB ASK
SC DHfK	Engelhard Gisela	SHB
SC Einheit Dresden	Steinert Gerd (ab 1.7. Kreissportarzt)	SHB
SC Karl-Marx-Stadt	Dr. Tolkmitt Ullrich	SHB
SC Turbine Erfurt	Dr. Tausch Horst	SHB
SC Chemie Halle	Dr. Franke Margot	SHB

STASI secret police files used in preparation for a national competition against the Soviet Union, describing the timing and dosages of drugs and designating the doctors responsible for administering them.

4b

Alle Eintragungen bei der Einweisung der
Sektionsärzte wurden in VD-Tsüdlerin vorgenommen. Nach Auskunft des IM sind im
wesentlichen alle Sektionsärzte vom Leiter der
SHB im jeweiligen Bezirk schriftlich verpflichtet.
Es ist jedoch empfehlenswert das durch die
Sportsachbearbeiter in den Bezirken" nachprüfen
zu lassen.
In den Clubs sind die Cheftrainer u. die betreffenden Trainer der ausgewählten Trainings-
gruppen eingeweilt. Die Cheftrainer wurden
1975 anläßlich der DDR-Meisterschaften in
Piesteritz vom Generalsekretär des Schwimm-
sportbandes der DDR VD-verpflichtet u.
auf die besondere Verantwortung bei der
Anwendung unterstützender Mittel hinge-
wiesen. Die Cheftrainer hatten ihrerseits den
Auftrag in gleicher Weise mit ihren Club-
trainern zu sprechen. Der IM informierte,
daß wir unbedingt unseren Einfluß
geltend machen, da erfahrungsgemäß

- die Verpflichtung der Trainer
  sehr oberflächlich durchgeführt
  wird u.

- unterdessen eine ganze Reihe
  Trainer gewechselt haben oder
  ausgeschieden sind bzw. durch
  neue ersetzt wurden

In den SHB's der Bezirke dürfen von den
genannten Maßnahmen nur

- der Leiter der SHB
- der stellv. Ltr. der SHB für Leistungssport
- u. der obengenannte Sektionsarzt

wissen.

STASI secret police files reporting on the organizational structure and protocol of the doping system, including directives to the trainers.

48

Prinzipien:

- Bei Sportlern unter 18 Jahren wird die legende Verabreichung von Vitaminen angewendet, d.h. alles geschieht ohne Wissen der Betreffenden.
- Sportler über 18 Jahren werden in die Problematik einbezogen u. vom Trainer mündlich zum Schweigen verpflichtet

Zielstellungen:

- individuelle Anstiegs- u. Abklingrate der zu verabreichenden Substanzen bei Männer u. Frauen prüfen
- Verhalten des körpereigenen Testosteronspiegels (männliches Sexualhormon) bei Männern testen u. prüfen inwieweit sich dies schädlich o. positiv auf die Leistungsentwicklung auswirkt.
- Verhalten der Maximalkraft – Wettkampfwerte u. welche Leistung möglich
- Feststellung der Laktatsenkung bei sportartspezifischen Tests (Dioktazt bei 8 x 200 m)
- bessere Erholungs- u. Belastungsverträglichkeit mit Präparat B 17 prüfen

Methode:

Zu bestimmten Terminen werden den Sportlern 5 ml. Blut und 10 ml. Urin abgenommen und zur speziellen Untersuchung dem FKS zugeleitet. Zusätzlich werden durch die Sektionsärzte u. Trainer schriftliche bzw. mündliche Einschätzungen und sportmethodische Tests vorgenommen. Die Laktatbestimmung erfolgt ausschließlich am FKS.

STASI secret police files regarding preservation of the secrecy of doping—athletes under eighteen years of age are not to be told what they are given, and all labels are to be removed from drugs prior to their being administered. Athletes eighteen years of age and older are to be orally advised that they are being given steroids, but are to be sworn to secrecy.

-5-

49

Im Prinzip werden diese Proben zu
folgenden Zeiten von einem PKW des FKS
abgeholt

Nordroute →
11.2. / 4.3. / ... 5.4. / 4.6. / 18.6.
(Halle, Magdeburg, Potsdam, Berlin)
Rostock ... S. selbst anliefern

Südroute →
6.0 ... 6.4. / 10.5. / 7.6. / 22.6.
(Dresden, K.-M.-Stadt, Erfurt)

Im wesentlichen soll die Ärztin Bornesfeld
mitfahren u. bei Sportlern zusätzliche Kontroll-
abnahmen machen, die nicht mit zum
ausgewählten Kaderstamm gehören, um zu ver-
hindern, daß die Sektionsärzte gemeinsam mit
den Trainern illegale Verabreichung von
Medikamenten vornehmen.

Zur Aufbewahrung der Medikamente durch
die Sektionsärzte wurden keine speziellen
Festlegungen getroffen, da sie in der Regel in
allen Apotheken gegen Rezept zu erhalten
sind.

STASI secret police files outlining the delivery plan for picking up athletes' urine samples for testing at the central laboratory.

—4—

zusätzlich Sportmethod.-Tests vom Trainer
zum Institut
Laktatbestimmung im SFB

Sportler:

SC Dynamo
  TGr. Warnatzsch ⟶

  Lehmann
  Koltsch
  Töpfer
  Schöne   } Männer
  Tauber
  Grätti
  Grabs

  TGr. Gläser / Krause ⟶

  Krause
  Pollak
  Nitzschke
  Altmann   } Frauen
  Schutt
  Matz
  Knacke
  Witt

TSC
  TGr. Hübner ⟶
  Wachenschwanz
  Lange
  Gansdrow   } Männer
  Gold
  Schwandt
  Hermann

STASI secret police files listing male and female athletes at Club Dynamo and Club TSC and their schedules for testing.

5.1

TGr. Matunek

Bedler
Hartmann   } Mädchen ... die endlez
Richter   } erst Ende Apr. entsch

SC Emp. Rostock

    TGr. Schleg. →

    58 Berger
    58 Klatte   } Männer
    59 M...
    60 ...ke

SE M

    Gr. Sack →

    57 Ackenhausen)
    58 Krüger   } Männer
    53 Mehlhase   )
    59 Schmidt   )

    TGr. Vorpagel →

    61 Stelle   } Mädchen

HSK

    TGr. Herberg →

    56 Wannja   )
    60 Fruicke   )
    53 Pawils   )
    54 Plesdike   } Männer
    60 Groboth   )
    59 Israel   )
    58 Mannschuß)
    58 Kriza   )
    53 Koff   )

STASI secret police files of sport clubs and their respective athletes.

-6-

SC DHfK

 TGr. König   →

  53 Schott   —⎱ Mädchen
  53 Engelmann ⎰
  53 Brückner
  60 Jank   ⎱ Mai entschl. ab
  61 Priemer ⎰ einbezogen

 TGr. Leopold →

  57 Paffel
  59 Lorenz ⎱ Männer
  60 Leopold ⎰
  Schlegel
  Löscher ⎱ nur Testosteron
  Klahn   ⎰

SC Einh Dresden

 TGr. Neumann ⎱
  53 Richter   ⎰ Mädchen
  60 Linke
  60 Treiber
  61 Mankisch

 TGr. Rosenkranz →

  58 Böhmert ⎱ Männer
  58 Schmidt ⎰

S

STASI secret police files listing male and female athletes and some of the drugs administered to them.

SC K-M-St

53

TGr. Kohles →

58 Tauber
61 Thümer
60 Wächtler
59 Wurdich
61 Fiebig

} Mädchen

TGr. Freyer

57 Beer
58 Gabor
Kühn
59 Schmoller

} Männer

SC Turb.

TGr. Fricke →

60 Wahrendorf
59 Kahle

} Mädchen

60 Stern
58 Schimmelda
59 Matthei

} Männer

SC Chemie Halle

TGr. Henneberg →

60 Jäger Regina
59 Schröder Günther

Aufbewahrung   Jeder wählt eigne Methode ?
Notizen über Gaben u.a. Dinge ←
VD Bücher

STASI secret police files listing athletes at various clubs.

INDEX

ABOUT THE AUTHOR

Dr. Steven Ungerleider, an author of four books, completed his undergraduate studies in psychology at the University of Texas, Austin, where he also competed as a collegiate gymnast. He holds master's and doctoral degrees from the University of Oregon and is a licensed psychologist at Integrated Research Services, Incorporated, in Eugene, Oregon. He is also an adjunct professor at the University of Oregon, in Eugene. Ungerleider has been the recipient of numerous federal grant awards and has published widely in the prevention and performance-enhancement literature. Since 1984 he has served on the United States Olympic Committee Sport Psychology Registry and has consulted with several college, Olympic, and professional sports organizations. In November 1991, Ungerleider was presented with the Distinguished Alumni Award from the University of Texas, Austin. In July 1992, Ungerleider's work was featured in *Psychology Today,* and he subsequently was named special correspondent for the magazine.

Ungerleider's books include *Beyond Strength* (McGraw-Hill, 1991, with coauthor Dr. Jacqueline Golding), which is a psychological study of depression, coping, resiliency, and response to stress among 1,200 Olympic athletes. His second book, *Quest for Success* (WRS/Spence Publications, 1994), is an in-depth profile of fifty Olympic athletes and their history of child abuse, family dysfunction, and ability to overcome odds to achieve success. *Mental Training for Peak Performance,* his third book (Rodale/St. Martin's Press, 1996), is now in its third printing and was named as a book-of-the-month-club selection for *Men's Health* magazine.

Ungerleider's work has been reviewed in *Elle, Longevity, Outside, Runner's World, Allure,* the *New York Daily News, San Francisco Chronicle, Boston Herald, Dallas Morning News,* and the *International Herald Tribune.* He was recently featured in the television special entitled *The Thrill of Sport and Speed,* aired on the A&E History Channel in late 1999.